2005

Ethics at Work

Daniel Terris

Ethics at Work

Creating Virtue in an American Corporation

Brandeis University Press

Waltham, Massachusetts

PUBLISHED BY UNIVERSITY PRESS OF NEW ENGLAND

HANOVER AND LONDON

Brandeis University Press

Published by University Press of New England,

One Court Street, Lebanon, NH 03766

www.upne.com

©2005 by Brandeis University

Printed in the United States of America

5   4   3   2   1

Library of Congress Cataloging-in-Publication Data

Terris, Daniel.
    Ethics at work : creating virtue in an American corporation / Daniel Terris.
        p.   cm.
    Includes bibliographical references and index.
    ISBN 1-58465-333-7 (cloth : alk. paper)
        1. Business ethics—United States.   2. Lockheed Martin Missiles & Space (Firm)   I. Title.
    HF5387.5.U6T47 2005
    174'.4—dc22   2005000917

For Maggie

Contents

Acknowledgments

The leaders and staff of the division of Ethics and Business Conduct at the Lockheed Martin Corporation provided me with access and assistance at every step of my research. They do not fully agree with the conclusions that I have drawn about their corporation, but I appreciate and admire the way that they were willing to subject their work to an outsider's scrutiny. Maryanne Lavan, Nancy Higgins, Joe Kale, Phil Tenney, and Bud Reid at corporate headquarters, and several ethics officers in various sites around the country gave generously of their time. My greatest debt at Lockheed Martin is to Brian Sears, the director of ethics awareness, who guided me through the process and accompanied me on my travels through the corporation.

Several individuals outside of Lockheed Martin helped orient me to the context of the corporation's work. Special thanks to Steve Cohen for introducing me to Lockheed Martin's ethics program, and to Mike Hoffman and Stuart Gilman for letting me test out my ideas and thinking on them at various points in the process. Mark Wilson, Leigh Swigart, and Michael Tierney took time out of their busy summers to read the manuscript and challenge me to improve it. Phyllis Deutsch of the University Press of New England provided astute commentary at key moments.

My terrific colleagues at the International Center for Ethics, Justice and Public Life at Brandeis University kept our work going while I was immersed in this project, and also kept me focused on the ultimate purposes of our common enterprise. The collective efforts of Kara Bayer, Melissa Blanchard, Cindy Cohen, Mari Fitzduff, Stephanie Gerber, Marci McPhee, Ian Richmond, Jennifer Rouse, and Leigh Swigart contributed in dozens of ways to this book. I also appreciate the support that I have received over the years from a series of provosts at Brandeis University—Irv Epstein, Mel Bernstein, and Marty Krauss—as well as from President Jehuda Reinharz.

My father, David Terris, was the first person to introduce me to the idea of corporate ethics: Presenting me with one share of stock each of Pacific Gas & Electric, Trans World Airlines, and Texaco as a present for my eighth birthday, he encouraged me to keep abreast of the companies' actions in the world, not just their stock prices. My mother, Susan Terris, encouraged and inspired me to write. These days, my four boys— Ben, Eli, Theo, and Sam—prod my thinking with provocative questions. Maggie Stern Terris is the center of my world.

Daniel Terris
January 2005

Ethics at Work

Introduction

In the Shadow of the Skunk Works

DAVE SANDERS MEETS me at the entrance of the Lockheed Martin facility in Palmdale, California, just outside the security office, the credit union, and the gift shop carrying toy models of U-2s and Stealth fighters.[1] An understated man in his fifties, Sanders is the site's full-time ethics officer, one of eighty men and women throughout the corporation charged with communicating and implementing the company's values. He greets me in the desert sunshine in shirtsleeves, and we spend a good part of the day touring the premises, stopping to chat with some of the employees on the line.

The Palmdale facility occupies dozens of acres of desert, in close proximity to the enormous expanse of Edwards Air Force Base. Once a manufacturing plant, Palmdale is now primarily a refitting facility, where Lockheed Martin installs up-to-date technology into some of its most venerable aircraft. In one enormous hangar, I climb into a C-130 cargo plane, now being retooled as a mobile, in-flight media station. Loaded with tons of new electronics, the plane will now be capable of flying halfway across the world to jam radio signals within a radius of hundreds of miles. The half-finished plane, with its crisscross of colorful wires, gleaming cables, and mysterious boxes, will one day have the mission of carrying the American message of liberty and opportunity to drown out enemy voices in the far corners of the globe.

The sleek bodies of the famous U-2 planes, with their distinctive pointed noses, dot another hangar. Rechristened the TR-1 after the U-2 became infamous, these planes, too, are being refitted with the latest space-age technology. After more than a year in Palmdale, they will emerge with even more sophisticated capacity to spy on earth from sixteen miles in the air, answering the call for better information, delivered more quickly, more precisely, more secretly. Later that morning, a flat, black, batlike craft glides through the desert haze and comes to rest on the tarmac. The Stealth fighter was one of Lockheed Martin's triumphs, the first plane capable of disappearing in midair, its jet-black surface jumbling radar signals and baffling those who scan the skies.

I am not allowed to bring a camera or a tape recorder with me on these rounds, and there is one part of the facility that I cannot visit at all. An unassuming jumble of buildings at Palmdale houses the current iteration of the Skunk Works. The top-secret design facility was moved to Palmdale when Lockheed closed its original headquarters in Burbank. Off limits even to most of those who work in other parts of Palmdale, the Skunk Works retains its aura of mystery and its reputation for developing the most sophisticated of the military's top-secret projects. To enter the Skunk Works is to enter the "black" world of aircraft and weaponry, whose products may not be seen, deployed, or even acknowledged for decades to come. The gift shop at the entrance to the facility sells caps with the jaunty little skunk logo on the bill.

Standing near the Skunk Works barracks and the U-2 hangars, I am in the shadow of the nerve center for some of the most innovative engineering projects accomplished in human history. I am also standing in a principal outpost of one of the largest enterprises in the United States, the corporation that does the most business with the U.S. Department of Defense, running to more than $20 billion in 2003 alone. Lockheed Martin is about big ideas, big products, and big business.

Amid the heavy machinery and the high-security fences, Dave Sanders moves comfortably, chatting casually with line employees and supervisors, moving in and out with ease, clearly a man known and liked and trusted in the facility. He has been in the ethics office for three years now, after a career in various aspects of human resource management. Ethics, he tells me, is not complicated. It's a matter of helping people see that doing the right thing is just as easy as doing it wrong. Sanders introduces me to the men and women who work on these planes, and who do their part for Lockheed Martin and, as they see it, for the United States of America. Much of his time, he tells me, is spent simply troubleshooting: resolving problems between a line worker and his supervisor; helping an employee receive a benefit she is owed; advising an executive on how to handle a client's gift. Sanders also oversees the annual ethics awareness program at Palmdale. Ethics awareness is a mandatory exercise for every

Lockheed Martin employee; one year everyone had to play a board game based on the *Dilbert* comic strip. Sanders sees himself as a specialist in prevention. No issue is too small; if a worker thinks a problem is an ethics issue, then it *is* an ethics issue, as far as he is concerned. Yes, he pursues investigations of wrongdoing as well: labor time charged incorrectly, or an accusation of harassment, or a violation of safety regulations. But by Sanders's lights, his facility is pretty clean. The expected dose of human frailty is contained and defused, he explains, by an ethics program that values the individual and rewards work done according to the company values.

Dave Sanders is the face of ethics at Lockheed Martin, and, in some ways, the face of corporate ethics in the United States today. Low-key, commonsense, and practical, Sanders also embodies a clear sense of mission, as he represents the corporation's neatly packaged and scrupulously documented program. He is part of a conscious and sustained effort to make ethics an integral part of Lockheed Martin's "value" as a corporation, crucial to its sales and recruiting efforts, as well as to its inner workings and its public image. Values and ethics now reinforce Lockheed Martin's image of a noble enterprise; innovation in delivering goodness is presented hand in hand with innovation in delivering space-age engineering.

Between 1999 and 2002, a series of dramatic scandals rocked corporate America. In their wake, writers and commentators rushed to examine "what went wrong" at Enron and WorldCom and Tyco and others. The tales of unbridled greed, the exposure of faulty systems of checks and balances, and the charges of poor public oversight gave impetus to the rapid development of programs in ethics and business conduct in corporations across the United States. The accounts of failure made a compelling case for the reexamination of the fundamentals of American business.

This book takes a different tack. Instead of focusing on failure, it begins with the premise that there might be something to learn from a corporation that has made a sustained and public commitment to ethics and values going back over two decades. It is a portrait of how one American corporation—Lockheed Martin—responded to scandal and has since continued to develop an ethics and business conduct program that involves hundreds of thousands of hours and millions of dollars each year.

This work is intended to contribute some sense of vitality and detail to discussions of corporate ethics, and to complement the rich trove of writings on ethics in American business: philosophical works that tease out the theory behind applied ethics; cautionary works that narrate stories of waste, fraud, and abuse; and practical works that advise business leaders on how to integrate ethics into their organizations. By simply describing the power and the limitations of one company's efforts, I hope to illustrate the complexities and challenges of developing and maintaining a corporate ethics program.

In conceiving this book, I have tried to address a series of straightforward questions:

- What led Lockheed Martin to develop its ethics program, and how did the program come to take so prominent a role in the corporation's public image?
- What does the corporation mean by "ethics," and how does it conceive of the goals of its ethics program?
- What activities have been implemented under the ethics banner?
- How well do those activities meet the goals it has set for itself in this area?
- Does the corporation's ethics program match public expectations of what it means to be a good corporate citizen in the United States?

In answering these questions, I have focused more on the design and execution of Lockheed Martin's ethics program than on its results. Assessments of a corporation's ethical *performance* are difficult and controversial, and they require much more access and data than I was granted as I conducted my research. The question of whether, in the largest sense, an extensive ethics program has made Lockheed Martin a more "ethical" corporation is, therefore, beyond the boundaries of this study. I am more interested, in any case, in the *choices* that the corporation has made in defining ethics and in creating activities to promote ethics as a part of its culture. Some of these choices respond effectively and powerfully to the challenges that the company faces. Other choices—

notably, the key questions that Lockheed Martin chooses to exclude from its ethics program—may leave the corporation vulnerable to future scandals and public disapprobation.

The defense industry has, to some people's surprise, the broadest and most sustained set of ethics programs of any sector of American business today. Lockheed Martin has built and maintained an extensive formal ethics and business conduct program since the mega-corporation was formed through a merger in 1995. The program builds on efforts first developed in the 1980s in the corporation's "heritage" companies— Lockheed, Martin Marietta, and parts of IBM, General Dynamics, and General Electric, among others. Defense contractors had responded to a series of crises—global scandals involving bribery, overcharging, and collusion—that severely undermined their public image and their standing with their biggest client, the U.S. government. Lockheed had been rocked by a sensational overseas bribery scandal in the 1970s; its new management was particularly eager to change the corporation's practice, image, and fortune. The company helped to found the Defense Industry Initiative, a consortium of companies that pledged to establish substantive programs to improve their integrity.

Defense contractors were among the first to initiate formal ethics programs in a big way, but a number of other developments stimulated attention to ethics throughout American business during the 1990s. Perhaps the single biggest "stick" was the development of federal sentencing guidelines for wrongdoing involving organizations, first put into effect in 1991 and strengthened several times since. The guidelines have for the first time made senior executives personally and legally responsible for fraud and abuse committed by their companies during their tenure, and they also created a series of benchmarks by which American corporations would be judged. Organizations that took specific steps to shore up ethics efforts would be treated less harshly when problems did surface. The 1991 guidelines specified that punishments of organizations found to be in violation of the law would be mitigated by the existence of "an effective compliance and ethics program." Of course there were positive incentives for attention to ethics as well. These included the benefits of an improved public image, the reciprocal goodwill of customers, and long-term efficiencies that came from eradicating waste and fraud.

The corporate scandals of the first years of the twenty-first century instigated additional federal measures that raised the bar for corporate ethics programs. In 2002, Congress passed the Sarbanes-Oxley Act, which tightened regulations regarding financial disclosures and conflict of interest, and which also increased penalties for certain types of white-collar crime.[2] Building on Sarbanes-Oxley, the U.S. Sentencing Commission (USSC) issued new sets of revised guidelines in 2003 and 2004. The 2003 guidelines dramatically increased the criminal penalties for executives whose white collar crimes affected a large number of people or endangered the solvency of publicly-traded companies. A defendant who shredded a substantial number of documents could spend more than three years in prison; an executive whose actions defrauded more than 250 employees or investors could face a sentence of more than ten years.

The 2004 USSC guidelines expanded and detailed the government's requirements for corporate compliance and ethics programs. The original 1991 organizational guidelines had included benchmarks for such programs; the 2004 guidelines added detail and raised standards, by requiring corporations to promote an "organizational culture" to encourage ethics and compliance with the law. That "organizational culture" would minimally require the knowledge and participation of the corporation's board and senior officers in the ethics program, the identification of specific individuals to operate the program, extensive training and communication about ethics throughout the workforce, and auditing and evaluation of the ethics and compliance efforts. In other words, it would no longer be sufficient simply to post the rules and regulations on a notice board, or to distribute an occasional memo about business conduct. Companies whose ethics programs were viewed as pro forma would be subject to more severe penalties than corporations that could credibly claim that they had woven ethics into the structure of their institutional life.[3]

These developments, among other things, heightened attention to business conduct and helped to stimulate a new cottage industry in the United States: the work of the ethics consultant. Lockheed Martin is part of an intricate web of peers, clients, and providers who have made ethics into a big business within big business. Amid the complexities of legal requirements, government regulations, and public expectations, various subfields emerged. Some consultants specialized in "compliance" with the law. Others focused on "ethical standards" that went beyond legal requirements. Others promoted a "values" approach that emphasized internal transformation rather than external pressures and incentives. Non-profits, for-profits, academics, philosophers, psychologists, marketers— the field was wide open to a variety of players who have helped reinvent and redefine ethics in the modern workplace. The cooperative arrangements between companies and consultants have put into place important new measures, but both parties also have sometimes had a vested interest in creating programs that place a premium on shiny surfaces rather than searching self-examination.

When the corporate ethics scandals made headlines, defense contractors could take some comfort in being ahead of the curve. They already had in place the basics: codes of conduct, corporation-wide awareness programs, investigative teams, incentives for right-minded behavior. These efforts, however, do not mean that the defense industry has entirely quelled illegal and unethical behavior. Lockheed Martin's own program was born on the heels of a 1995 settlement involving a bribery scandal, which had developed after Lockheed had begun its ethics initiatives. (Note that "Lockheed" refers to the Lockheed Corporation before its 1995 merger with Martin Marietta; the merged corporation is "Lockheed Martin.") More recently, the Boeing Corporation was rocked by two simultaneous but unrelated scandals—one involving document theft (from Lockheed Martin, no less), and the other involving a high-ranking Air Force officer's conflict of interest. Boeing's chief financial officer, who was directly implicated, was summarily fired, and its chief executive officer resigned in December 2003. During the Iraq War, alleged abuses at Halliburton, once run by Vice-President Dick Cheney, took center stage.

These particular incidents aside, the defense industry also raises special concerns as a sector whose products and business interests themselves are controversial within American society. The sheer size of the industry invites exploitation and the misuse of power. The web of relationships between corporate leaders and high-ranking government officials offers ample opportunity for foul play, as multi-billion-dollar deals are made and broken. And, of course, defense contractors make weapons, whose presence and use raise a host of questions about the morality of defense, warfare, and violence.

So what *has* been accomplished in fifteen years of persistent ethics initiatives at the defense giants? What difference does the work of an ethics officer like Dave Sanders make? What does "ethics" mean in this context anyway? I was curious to explore these questions in depth within a single organization, to try to make more sense of the promise and the perils of making a substantial commitment to an ethics program.

In 1998, shortly after I became director of the International Center for Ethics, Justice, and Public Life at Brandeis University, my colleague Jerry Samet from the philosophy department dropped into my office. He was carrying a bright yellow board-game box, marked in bold letters with the words "Ethics Challenge." He opened up the box and showed me a board with stations something like the old game of "Clue," only there were brightly drawn characters from the comic strip *Dilbert* lurking by the "Cooler" and in the "Boss's office." Samet told me that he had chipped in some ideas for this game, which had been developed by some friends of his in the consulting business in downtown Boston, and he thought that people at a Brandeis center with some concern about ethics might be interested. The "Ethics Challenge," he said, had been developed for the defense industry giant, Lockheed Martin. Each year, every one of the company's 130,000 employees played the game.

The "Ethics Challenge" sat on my bookshelf for several years. We played the game at the center instead of having a staff meeting one week, and I tried it out in a couple of undergraduate classes. Visitors to my office would spy the bright yellow box, open it up, shuffle through the *Dilbert* cards, and chuckle appreciatively. Every so often, Jerry Samet would call me up and ask whether I had followed up with his friends who had developed the game.

Then the wave of corporate scandals hit the American business world. The spectacular implosions of Enron, WorldCom, Tyco, and a host of other giant concerns touched off inquiries and investigations that focused on mismanagement and wrongdoing. These also brought renewed attention to the question of how American corporations had failed to address ethics effectively within their organizations. How had they neglected ethics so completely that billions of dollars went up in smoke?

I found myself interested in the opposite question: What *were* American corporations doing to address ethics? In particular, I was interested in institutions that made a sustained and visible commitment to ethics and values as an integral part of their organizational culture. By "sustained," I meant institutions that had been doing ethics seriously and consciously for at least a decade. By "visible," I meant that an organization was confident enough about its program to stake its reputation on claims about its integrity. By "organizational culture," I meant that the ethics effort was widely diffused, somehow touching the lives and work of individuals at every level of the institution. Now that the U.S. Sentencing Commission guidelines had given the idea of "organizational culture" such prominence, these questions were more compelling than ever.

As I was mulling these questions over, the "Ethics Challenge" game box caught my eye. I called Jerry Samet and told him that I was ready to follow up. I was ready to learn how a corporate giant like Lockheed Martin went about its ethics program.

My inquiry started in the downtown Boston offices of Convergent Learning, the successor to the consulting firm that had worked with Lockheed Martin to develop the original "Ethics Challenge." There I met Steve Cohen, who in turn introduced me to Joe Kale, a senior Lockheed Martin ethics executive who soon went on to become the ethics business area director for the new Integrated Systems & Solutions (ISS) unit of the corporation. Kale is tall, lean, and neatly dressed, with the gentle manner of an understanding clergyman or the ideal coach for your son's Little League team. He explains things patiently, but never pedantically. "Here's a guy who lives and breathes ethics," Steve Cohen told me. "This is a guy who plays the 'Ethics Challenge' at home with his kids . . . and his kids are five and three!"

Joe Kale sketched out the history of Lockheed Martin's ethics efforts. Beginning in the 1980s, many companies in the defense industry began ethics programs, under pressure from the U.S. government following a series of scandals. After a wave of mergers and acquisitions created Lockheed Martin as a single corporation in 1995, the company invested heavily in consolidating and expanding those earlier efforts, so that ethics was not only central to the Lockheed Martin culture, but a crucial element in creating a common identity for a widely scattered organization. The new Lockheed Martin, after all, included divisions that manufactured, repaired, and outfitted sophisticated aircraft, other divisions focused on information technology, and dozens of other types of services related to aircraft and modern weaponry. The "Ethics Challenge" was only one of many efforts undertaken by the corporation's sixty-five ethics officers that attempted to bring a common sense of values to divisions and employees working in widely different circumstances. Kale invited me to take a closer look.

I traveled to Lockheed Martin's headquarters in Bethesda, Maryland, where I negotiated permission for access to the company's facilities and materials in order to conduct the research. Such inquiries are obviously a delicate matter, not only because any large corporation is sensitive about its image, but because so many of Lockheed Martin's operations involve projects related to national security. Eventually I worked out a formal agreement that allowed me to conduct the research under the watchful eye of Brian Sears, the corporation's "director of ethics awareness." I could visit company facilities and conduct interviews with Sears's permission and in his company, and the corporate ethics office would share the materials that it used as a part of its work. Lockheed Martin would have the right to review the manuscript to ensure that I was not disclosing proprietary information or compromising national security, but otherwise the company would have no control over the book's content. Naturally, I would have preferred to work with fewer restrictions, but I also appreciated Lockheed Martin's willingness to cooperate at all. Keeping my options open, I had approached another defense industry giant, Raytheon, with a similar proposal. Raytheon turned me down, anxious about the uncertainties of exposing its operation to the scrutiny of an outsider. Unlike their competitors, the people involved with Lockheed Martin's ethics program had the courage and the confidence to let an outsider peer in.

My research at Lockheed Martin took me to a number of the company's facilities and activities in Maryland, Virginia, Florida, and California, as well as to the corporation's annual ethics officer conference in Orlando, Florida. I have spoken with dozens of ethics officers, as well as employees who are the "customers," so to speak, of the company's ethics program. Joe Kale and Brian Sears have sent me boxes of ethics program materials, dating back to the earliest Lockheed Martin efforts in 1995 and 1996, and I have had a chance to witness the annual ethics awareness program in action. Explaining my project, I told every Lockheed Martin employee I talked with that I would be trying to paint a fair and accurate portrait of the company's ethics program, and that I would also be asking tough questions about the ultimate value of the corporation's ethics effort both to Lockheed Martin itself and to the larger world. I have tried to be faithful to that explanation in writing this book.

Two genres dominate the market of contemporary books about corporate ethics in America: narratives of scandal, and prescriptions for avoiding them. The tales of fraud and abuse focus, for the most part, on the actions of corrupt corporate leaders. They portray organizations whose cultures have permitted a small number of individuals to perpetrate various types of fraud on a hitherto unthinkable scale. The emphasis of these books, some by former insiders, is on greed in its crudest form: greed abetted by new technologies, by the speculative quality of the American economy, and by the laxity of colleagues. These are cautionary tales; their moral, by and large, is the vulnerability of large-scale modern organizations to calculated deception by a small number of clever people determined to put their own interests ahead of every other stakeholder.[4]

At the same time, books and articles have been published with the intent of helping corporate leaders figure out how to implement ethics programs that will engender public confidence, avoid lawsuits, and create a sense of integrity throughout the enterprise. These books pay some attention to the excesses of individuals, but they are focused more closely on the culture of businesses as a whole. These prescriptive books take as their starting point a variety of disciplinary contexts—philosophy, management, economics, organizational behavior, to name a few—to provide vocabulary and strategies for heading off scandal while maintaining profits. Some of these works are intensely practical in nature, providing specific advice for companies looking to create or transform their ethics programs, and using contemporary companies as models.[5] A particularly useful approach has identified the broad acceptance of the idea of a corporate "personality," and suggests models for corporations to think of ethics and the long-term health of the company as symbiotic components of the corporate enterprise.[6] These works differ greatly in their methodology and their prescriptions, but they share a common didactic purpose: to provide a clear road map for organizational leaders who wish to make ethics a central part of their institutional culture.

Tales of scandal and prescriptions for change are not the only types of books that have emerged in recent years. Some thinkers and researchers have focused more on the "experience" of work, and the quest for meaning within the life of an organization. These writings treat ethics as the outcome of "good work": Individual and organizational character is strengthened if the mission of an organization is clear, if workers have maximum opportunity for growth, and if the larger social conditions allow corporations to thrive without resorting to underhanded tactics. Some have focused more on personal transformation, building on the idea that institutional ethics has to begin with the passion and commitment and investment of professionals and leaders within the organization.[7] Other observers have focused their attention on the nature of work itself, from a conviction that the "alignment" of an organization with its mission is the most solid basis for the development of both an ethical and a productive institutional culture.[8] These texts embrace an understanding of ethics that goes beyond adherence to principles and that includes an examination of the complete role that individuals play within an organizational setting.

Many of these books offer case studies as illustrations of a larger point. This book draws on some of the ideas that these authors have developed, in the context of a focused, descriptive look at a single corporation's efforts. With these other works in mind, let me say a few things that this book is *not*.

This book is not an "authorized" account of Lockheed Martin's ethics program. Yes, the corporation reserved the right to review the manuscript, but only to make sure that I was not disclosing any company or federal secrets. Many Lockheed Martin employees were generous with time and assistance, but without expectation that I would tell their story the way that it might be told on their own web site or by their own public relations department. When attending company events, I paid my own way, and I accepted no favors, other than the materials of the ethics and business conduct department itself.

Moreover, this book is not connected to any consulting work done with Lockheed Martin or any other corporation. There is, as I have indicated, an extensive literature about applied ethics in American businesses written by people who are themselves consultants to corporations on how to develop and improve their ethics programs. I am not in that business, nor is anyone connected with the center that I direct at Brandeis. (We do offer programs that encourage judges and other professionals to reflect on ethics and values, using literature as the basis of discussion.) I did not enter the project with a particular method to advance, nor do I offer one here.

This project, then, does not begin with a bias in favor of a particular approach to corporate ethics, but it also does not begin with an attitude of cynicism. Some critics of business and weapons makers begin with the premise that big corporations in the United States, or companies in the defense industry, are inherently corrupt. I began this project by accepting at face value the idea that an ethics program in an American defense giant could be developed and promoted in good faith.

Finally, this book is not focused on scandal. Many recent books have told the stories of corporate fraud and abuse on a massive scale. Lockheed Martin has avoided a major ethics scandal since 1995. The ethics officers point to the success of their program. Critics of the company nevertheless point to a series of lower profile allegations, lawsuits, and government investigations that have not made national headlines. In any case, I have not undertaken investigative work in search of dishonest practices. Instead, I have focused on the ethics program as the company has designed it, so some questions about the ultimate impact of that program will have to be left to other investigators and to future historians.

This book *is* an attempt to present a fair but tough-minded look at what one major corporation actually does in its ethics program. I present the history of the corporation's ethical lapses, and the measures that it has taken in recent years to redress them. I have tried to understand what Lockheed Martin believes that it is accomplishing in its ethics program. I do not accept all of the company's premises about what an ethics program should achieve, but I have offered my ideas alongside the company's own perspective.

In this book, American history and culture serves as the backdrop and the screen against which my thoughts about Lockheed Martin are projected. This account could just as easily rely on the study of ethics (theoretical or applied) or organizational behavior or even sociology or anthropology. But I come to this project by way of an interest in how the currents of American history and literature continue to shape contemporary life. One reason that I rely on history is because, although the vocabulary has changed many times, Americans have been concerned about business ethics since the first Europeans arrived in New England, and attention to corporate behavior has been a steady feature of American life in the centuries since. Writers on corporate values sometimes construct a "pre-ethics" period in American life, when citizens and business leaders alike allegedly believed that business was an inherently amoral enterprise, that profit was the only motivating force, and that violations of the law or moral standards were greeted with a shrug. While it is true that brigands, outlaws, and robber barons in the business world operated with more impunity in earlier eras, it does not follow that Americans were indifferent to their behavior, nor does this mean that efforts to curtail fraud and greed in industry were negligible. Indeed, the complex interplay between business leaders, the government, the media, and the public over appropriate conduct in economic life has been a dominant theme since the middle of the nineteenth century, when industrialization began to change the American landscape. The arguments developed over the century and a half since then serve as the foundation for understanding of and response to contemporary conditions. I prefer to ground this book in the context of the ideals and expectations of the culture in which one institution has thrived.

I have identified here strands of thought about the business ethics that have developed in the American context. I do so in order to try to distinguish among very different sets of ideas and priorities that Americans have embraced with regard to these issues. My point is that one important source for the principles and practice of business ethics in contemporary American life is the traditions of the past. History is not by any means the only source; philosophy, the lived experience of corporate life, values embodied in religion or cultivated within families, and even common sense all play important roles. But the trajectory of time and memory exercises an important hold on contemporary attitudes, especially among those who take pride in implementing ethics programs that work in practice, not just in theory.

Essentially, I argue in this book that a group of decent, well-meaning people at Lockheed Martin has created an ethics program that is ambitious but incomplete. Few other institutions in American life have invested so much in ethics, and the program's success in making ethics a part of the regular consciousness of tens of thousands of company employees is impressive. Discussion of issues like conflict of interest, proprietary information, and various forms of harassment is deeply ingrained in the corporation's culture. Although it sometimes raises hackles of cynicism (or even provokes angry and violent reactions), the ethics program has been widely successful in promoting confidence in the company's integrity.

Yet the program is also hollow, because it defines ethics so narrowly that it deliberately ignores some of the largest questions about the company's policies and practices. Major questions about company policies, employment practices, the nature of the corporation's business, and fairness in the workplace are at the margins in Lockheed Martin's ethics program. These strict boundaries mean that the program is focused more on ensuring the integrity of individual actors, rather than ensuring that the corporation as a whole refrains from doing harm. I make no judgments here about the ethical *results* of Lockheed Martin's policies, products, and impact on the greater world. But I am concerned that by excluding these questions from its ethics program, Lockheed Martin may eventually make itself vulnerable to new and unforeseen types of scandals. As Americans take an ever broader and more critical view of corporate ethics, companies that define ethics too narrowly will do so at their peril.

I begin in chapter 1 by tracing several strands of thought about business ethics as they have developed over the course of the history of the United States. Americans have often talked at cross-purposes about the behavior of corporations, because their judgments have been informed by very different fundamental assumptions both about what exactly a right-minded company should do and about what exactly shapes a company's actions. I examine the image of the American tycoon as it emerged in the nineteenth and early twentieth centuries, drawing on literature to illustrate a national ambivalence about the magnetism and the greed of powerful leaders. Corporate ethics looks very different, however, when examined in the light of how businesses (as opposed to individuals) treat one another, or how companies treat their employees, or the impact of corporations on their communities. Each of these strands of thought has deep roots in the American past, and each leads to different conclusions and judgments about the present.

Chapter 2 focuses on a different aspect of history: the story of Lockheed Martin. The twenty-first-century mega-corporation is an amalgamation of dozens of companies in the aircraft and defense industries. I focus particularly on the portion that was Lockheed itself, a company with an exciting history of innovation in air and space travel. Amelia Earhart and Charles Lindbergh, among other legendary pilots, made record-breaking flights in some of the company's early models. The company's top-secret "Skunk Works" laboratory designed some of the most famous planes of World War II and the postwar era, including the U-2 and the Stealth fighter. But Lockheed was also beset by scandals, beginning as early as the 1950s, and by the 1980s, it had developed a notorious legacy of bribery, overcharging, and other shady business practices. The company's modern ethics program was born in the late 1980s, as the entire defense industry struggled to revive its reputation. The ethics program's scope broadened considerably when Lockheed and Martin Marietta merged in 1995, on the heels of yet another overseas bribery scandal.

Chapter 3 gives a detailed account of the various aspects of Lockheed Martin's ethics program. I treat the company's code of ethics, the role of its corps of ethics officers, the nature of internal ethics investigations, efforts to "sell" ethics to the employee community, and innovative programs like the corporation's annual "Ethics Film Festival." I also describe how Lockheed Martin measures its own success in the ethics area, through a biennial survey, and the struggles of the ethics program to maintain credibility within a bottom-line environment. This chapter focuses on the strengths of Lockheed Martin's ethics program, within the corporation's own definition of the program's mission.

Finally, in chapter 4, I raise a series of questions about Lockheed Martin's ethics program in the light of the very different ideas about business ethics that I describe earlier in the book. Lockheed Martin's ethics program is, in a way, gloriously democratic, in that it focuses on the responsibility of each and every individual in the corporation for the ethical dimension of his or her actions. On the other hand, this focus on individual behavior and this focus on ethics across the corporation tend to divert attention from collective decision making. The program can tackle egregious ethical lapses (like bribery or giving away company secrets) or minor breaches (like using company computers for entertainment or a personal business), but it seldom addresses the ramifications of decisions made by people in teams or policies set by senior managers and company leaders. As a result, Lockheed Martin's ethics program is all but silent on some of the major issues that have rocked American industry in recent years: accounting practices, fairness in employment policies, executive compensation, and the global impact of a company's core business. The company believes that these matters fall outside the scope of the ethics program, that they are dealt with in other venues. I argue, however, that the creation of strict boundaries around what constitutes an ethics issue inevitably dilutes the program, and may leave the corporation vulnerable to scandal. The corporation asserts that it is contributing to the common good by producing products that defend the American way of life. Its ethics program, however, avoids searching questions about Lockheed Martin's contributions to the common good, and so, in the end, I argue that it falls short of realizing its full potential to shape the corporation's impact on the country and the world in which we live.

chapter one

Titans and Warhogs

AMERICANS HAVE SHOWN concern about the moral behavior of businesses and business leaders since the earliest years of European settlement in the New World. Even while the United States developed the world's most productive capitalist environment, ideas about what constituted appropriate behavior in the business community became part of the national conversation. The term "business ethics" did not gain currency until the middle of the twentieth century, but long before that, a series of ideas and opinions about the appropriate limits on corporate activity had developed strong traditions. These traditions developed alongside the ideology of a laissez-faire free-market economy that emerged in the nineteenth century. In some ways these traditions regarding business behavior took their strength from the individualist tendency in American life; in other ways, they drew more on ideas about the common good that had their roots in religion. The emerging corporations of the nineteenth and early twentieth centuries did not, of course, always operate in accord with those traditions; indeed, the relative weakness of government allowed them a lot of latitude. Nevertheless, they operated in an environment where, at the very least, corporate leaders were compelled to make a public case that they ran enterprises that not only made money for the principals but also contributed to the common good.

Different people and groups emphasized different aspects of business behavior. So what has emerged over the course of American history is not a single, indivisible conception of what we now call business ethics, but a cluster of interwoven strands of thought. Contemporary attitudes about corporate malfeasance are profoundly affected by the ways in which earlier Americans have responded to successive waves of corporate scandal over the last two centuries. By sorting out these strands, and by examining the legacy that each has left for our own time, we are better positioned to evaluate in a comprehensive way the ethics programs of major corporations like Lockheed Martin.

An understanding of these strands of thought is important because, in the end, corporations cannot themselves choose the standards on which their ethics programs will be judged. Lockheed Martin, as an engineering company, is good at measuring things, and its leadership cares a great deal about measuring success. This attitude applies to its ethics program, as much as to airplane, missile, and software design. Its ethics officers are constantly challenged to produce data that show the value of the program, and offer specific suggestions for improvement. How can we judge the success of this "ethical culture"? One measure, which Lockheed Martin's ethics staff embraces, is that the corporation has managed to avoid a banner-headline scandal since 1995, when the merger of Lockheed and Martin Marietta formed the corporation in its current guise. In an era when other major corporations—including some of Lockheed Martin's largest competitors in the defense industry—have fallen prey to major scandals, this is no small achievement. Avoiding major scandals and earning the trust of the U.S. government are two important markers, but they are not sufficient.

Ultimately, corporations are judged in the court of public opinion, which takes the broad view of the subject of business ethics. Lockheed Martin makes large claims for its ethics program, and for the place of values within its corporate culture. The company puts a premium on "the personal integrity of each of our employees and their commitment to the highest standards of personal and professional conduct that underlie the ethical culture of Lockheed Martin." [1] A corporation may do a spectacular job of rooting out corruption, strengthening the moral fiber of its workforce, and associating itself with worthy social service projects, but if a small cabal of its senior executives succumbs to greed, or if its operations systematically despoil the environment, the company's claims to excellence in "ethics" will mean little.

By looking at history, I am arguing that the "court of public opinion" is not a shallow, fickle, ill-considered instrument of taste. It is, instead, a distillation of ideas and standards that have long and distinguished roots in American culture. A corporation's ethics programs may satisfy a philosopher, or a management specialist, or even its customers. But it also needs to respond to the full complement of traditional expectations, established and articulated by leaders in business, government, the media, the arts, and other actors in public life.

This is especially true for defense contractors, who are, after all, part of a quasi-governmental industry. Lockheed Martin and its competitors are owned by individual private investors, but a significant proportion of their work responds to a public activity, the nation's capacity to defend itself and to wage war. In some ways this quasi-governmental status gives them an edge in the public eye; they are able to bask in the glow of patriotism and the refracted glory of contributing to the military strength of a democratically elected government. In other ways, however, defense contractors come under especially intense scrutiny, from critics of the U.S. government's military policies, from skeptics about the "military–industrial complex," and from a general public that balks at the idea that corporations might be making exorbitant profits at the taxpayers' expense.

Flagrant corporate greed seems easy to spot and easy to label, but on closer examination it turns out that there are a number of competing and overlapping definitions of business ethics. Or, more precisely, there are several competing analyses of corporate behavior, which lead to different accounts of the standards to which companies should be held, the reasons that they violate those standards, and the remedies for the violations.

In this chapter I offer a small number of illustrations of five "strands of thought" that have emerged over the past 200 years. I am not attempting to paint a comprehensive history of American attitudes toward corporate ethics. My purpose is more modest. I mean only to suggest, through a selective look at aspects of American history, that the extent of historical scrutiny and activity regarding business practices has helped to create a climate where companies are expected to consider ethics in its broadest dimensions. In order to give a quick picture of the landscape, I summarize these five strands of thought briefly here, before turning to a fuller exploration of each in the balance of the chapter:

1. The sins of the tycoon. The oldest and most persistent conception of business ethics in the United States focuses on the actions and motivations of individual actors: the titans of the business world. This strand of thinking rests on the assumption that corporate entities are extensions of the character of their leaders. Corporate leaders acquire power, and then they can use it for good or for ill. These leaders are public men and women playing leadership roles in American society, so there is little distinction between ethics in their corporate capacity and ethics in their private lives. Americans have traditionally been ambivalent about the tycoons of business; admiration for their power and achievements has often softened public judgment of their foibles. This conception of business ethics leads naturally to a crisp and simple remedy for scandal: Replace the chief executive officer (CEO), and trust in the character of the next generation of leadership.

2. Business conduct. A second conception of business ethics focuses principally on how corporations conduct themselves according to the rules of their industry. The focus here is less on the behavior of individuals, but on how corporate entities act in relation to one another. This conception emerged in the middle years of the nineteenth century, as American industry developed and the frenzied atmosphere of growth and opportunity encouraged companies to cut moral corners in competing with one another. Price fixing, stock watering, aggressive underpricing— these kinds of tactics ultimately affect consumers and the society as a whole, but their immediate impact is felt within the corporate world itself. In our own day, this conception of corporate ethics falls roughly under the rubric of "business conduct," and it focuses less exclusively on the actions of the top management and more broadly on the various corporate practices that may violate laws or organizational values.

3. Putting workers first. Some people have been inclined to judge a corporation's ethics principally on how it treats its employees and on the equity and justice that it practices within. In this conception, the relationship between labor and management is at the crux of a corporation's moral stature. This standard of corporate behavior became prominent in the second half of the nineteenth century, as the great labor battles in steel and other industries called attention to exploitation of the American worker. In the twentieth century, attention to company policies on working hours, diversity, and gender issues has further complicated this issue. While criticism of corporate labor practice has been a persistent strand in American thinking, we should also pay attention to ways that some companies have tried to instill an "ethical culture" among their workers through active efforts to impose company values on the private lives of their employees.

4. Social responsibility. A fourth conception of business ethics places priority on the impact of a company on the local, national, and (in more recent times) the international communities of which it is a part. This strand of thinking pays most attention to the corporation as a public actor. The impact of industry on the natural environment was the starting point. In our own era, the notion of "corporate social responsibility" takes into account a host of environmental, economic, and social factors, as well as the impact of business on democratic government in the United States and abroad. What began as assessment of the impact of companies on their immediate environment now also includes an examination of corporations as global players.

5. The perils of profits. No treatment of business ethics in the United States is complete without a consideration of that small but influential band of Americans that has offered a persistent critique of the moral shortcomings of the profit motive itself. Capitalism by its nature generates a tension between equality and liberty, so skepticism about profits runs through the thinking of Americans of all political stripes concerned about the contours of a just society. Given our attention to Lockheed Martin, it is particularly interesting to examine attitudes over the course of United States history toward profits generated by weaponry and war.

These conceptions of business ethics are clearly not mutually exclusive. Adherents of "corporate social responsibility," for example, are certainly concerned about labor issues overseas, and some are vocal critics both of individual corporate leaders and of the profit motive itself. Yet I believe that these conceptions represent different enough starting points and emphases that they lead to different vocabularies, different standards of judgment, and very different conclusions about moral performance. One person may hold up a corporation as a sterling example of corporate ethics because it has diligently addressed its history of bribery and fraud, while another person may be excoriating the same company for the heartless manner in which it laid off workers by the thousand.

It should be said, at the beginning, that American opinion on all these strands of thinking has always been complex. Ambivalence about the country's powerful engines of economic growth has been an American way of life for more than 200 years. Keen and biting judgments about corporate greed go hand in hand with admiring encomiums for the power and ingenuity and energy of the most ruthless exploiters. This ambivalence also explains a great deal about the contemporary business climate. In the early years of the twenty-first century, the scandals continue to pop up with stunning regularity, thanks in part to American willingness simultaneously to voice public critique and harbor secret admiration.

An important goal for every corporation that is undertaking an ethics program in a serious way is to convince the broader public of the depth and effectiveness of its work in this area. More importantly, ethics programs have to be deep and strong enough to address the *next* crisis, not just the ones that a corporation has suffered or weathered in the recent past.

The Sins of the Tycoons

In 1653, Robert Keayne began to write his will. A prosperous merchant in the Massachusetts Bay Colony, Keayne used the occasion of his final testament for more than disposing of his estate. The document, which eventually ran to more than 51,000 words, was an elaborate account and justification of his commercial dealings in Puritan New England. Over the course of his career in Massachusetts, Keayne had been accused on numerous occasions of extracting too much profit from his fellow colonists; in one of the most vigorously disputed incidents, he was accused of marking up six-penny nails to eight and even ten pence per pound. For these and other similar matters, he had been tried formally in courts of law as well as informally in the court of public opinion, eventually attracting the attention of even such a worthy as Massachusetts governor John Winthrop for his "corrupt practice."[2]

Keayne's anguished "apologia" stands near the beginning of the story of how Americans have fixed on the moral character of leading businessmen as the ultimate measure of business ethics. Like many others after him, Robert Keayne pursued profits through what he considered classic Puritan virtues, like discipline and thrift, only to find himself (as he saw it) both rewarded for his prominence and castigated for his success. He lived in one of the most prestigious houses in colonial Boston, and he served the colony in a variety of appointed posts, yet his neighbors frequently judged his very prosperity as evidence of greed, heartlessness, and betrayal of his faith.

One of the challenges for Keayne and other business leaders of his day was to try to establish just what constituted ethical behavior in an era of shifting standards and vigorous moral and theological dispute. In Keayne's day, for example, some of New England's most prominent ministers were impassioned opponents of "usury," which at that time meant accepting any interest on a loan of money. But the view was losing ground to a rising tide of acceptance, even among Puritan clerics. Charging interest on a loan to the poor was still unacceptable, but a consensus was developing that interest-bearing loans between the better classes were an engine of economic growth, and therefore acceptable in furthering God's plans.[3] The success of a merchant was ultimately measured not just by how much wealth he acquired, but by how nimbly he was able to situate his business dealings within the context of disputed moral precepts. Keayne's story is an early iteration of one of the continuing themes in the story of American business leaders. Admired for their success, American leaders of industry have tended to equate their wealth with righteousness, believing that the success of their competitive tactics justified them morally as well as economically. For a time, public opinion supported their self-assessments—until changing standards of business practice exposed their deficiencies.

By the time Benjamin Franklin was making his fortune as a printer in eighteenth-century Philadelphia, the strict local control of the theocracy was a thing of the past, but Franklin was no less zealous than the Puritan divines in declaring the connection between commercial success and his version of the moral life. Franklin famously counseled young men to develop habits of temperance, thrift, discipline, and industry, keeping track by means of a literal moral ledger, a written account of their virtues and their foibles. More important, however, was Franklin's insistence on the *appearance* of virtue: A reputation for moderation and integrity, based on well-timed acts of kindness and charity, was for the printer an indispensable business asset.

Treating ethics as a matter principally of personal habit and outward appearance, Franklin encouraged Americans to judge their leaders—in business and otherwise—by public manifestations of character, rather than by the ins and outs of their financial dealings. This is not to say that Franklin exactly countenanced fraud or theft, but his moral system was based on weights and balances, so that failings in one department (let's say, shady financial dealings) might be offset by strong performance in another (spending money wisely, perhaps, or donating conspicuously to local institutions for the improvement of the poor). Business ethics, for Franklin, was the glittering example of a man's public character, and the sum total of his contribution to his society. It is perhaps only slightly unfair to Franklin to suggest that in his influential scheme, the obscure but honest merchant is less "ethical" than the wealthy philanthropist whose fortune was enhanced through the occasional bribe.

In the nineteenth century, American attention to the character of its business leaders hit its full stride. Indeed, the question became unavoidable, as the titans of the industrial era developed economic networks on a scale unimaginable to the Puritans and the Founding Fathers. The growth of the nation and the industrial revolution fostered enormous economic enterprises that came to be seen, fairly or not, as living embodiments of their bold and (sometimes) ruthless founders. John Jacob Astor's American Fur Company exploited the vast frontiers and made its founder the owner of great swaths of the developing metropolis of New York City. Cornelius Vanderbilt made several fortunes through steamships and railroads. Andrew Carnegie in steel, John Rockefeller in oil, J. P. Morgan in banking—the names of the founders became synonymous not only with their companies but with entire industries.

Making their way in a highly competitive (and unregulated) era, these early corporate leaders used a variety of unscrupulous means to build their fortunes, and widespread public criticism followed in their wake. Vanderbilt forced competitors in the railroad industry to conform to his will by refusing to ship their goods until his demands were met. (Asked later why he did not simply sue his competitors, the "Commodore" replied, "The law, as I view it, goes too slow for me when I have the remedy in my own hands."[4]) Carnegie was painted as the picture of evil for his company's forceful suppression of striking steel workers. Rockefeller's Standard Oil created its own economic climate by simply swallowing up competitors and thereby becoming the principal target of antitrust legislation.

These titans faced at times withering public criticism of their financial dealings, but they also succeeded to a great extent in persuading the American public to follow and adapt Benjamin's Franklin system of moral balance in judging their business ethics. Andrew Carnegie and John D.

Rockefeller, in particular, sold themselves as men of character who happened to make huge fortunes, and they made strategic philanthropic commitments that fortified their reputation for virtuous contributions to their communities and to the nation. Carnegie's writings on the "Gospel of Wealth" made a case for the moral efficacy of philanthropy, through which a rich man can become "the mere agent and trustee for his poorer brethren, bringing to their service his superior wisdom, experience, and ability to administer, doing for them better than they would or could do for themselves."[5] Rockefeller gave millions to foundations bearing his name and those of his family members, having secured his personal fortune before the company he founded was finally fragmented through antitrust law in 1911.

The titans' philanthropic enterprises did not entirely distract the American public from their sharp business practices. But the sheer scale of their enterprises—in both the for-profit and the nonprofit world—attracted ambivalent admiration. Their identification with the public impact of their work inevitably encouraged critics to think about business ethics in terms of personal character. This provided an easy target for caricature and criticism, but it also tended to temper harsh judgments. Their shortcomings, after all, were merely human failings.

American ambivalence about the character of its business leaders was expressed most richly in the work of its novelists. Occasionally, American culture has given birth to an unadulterated portrait of heartless greed, like the aptly named Gordon Gecko in Oliver Stone's film *Wall Street*. But more often American writers balanced the moral scales of their businessmen characters by calculating the personal cost of financial success. In *The Rise of Silas Lapham*, William Dean Howells portrayed a nouveau-riche paint manufacturer from rural New England who is slowly ground down by the social and economic pressures of his decision to settle his family in Boston. Abraham Cahan described the bittersweet side of the immigrant success story in *The Rise of David Levinsky*, in which the penniless arrival becomes a wealthy garment manufacturer, only to discover that he has abandoned the sources of meaning and pleasure that he had once found in the (unprofitable) study of Jewish texts. Joe Stecher, another successful immigrant character, makes the transition from labor to management in the printing industry in William Carlos Williams's *In the Money*; Stecher is emotionally torn by having to break a workers' strike in the plant where he once toiled. F. Scott Fitzgerald gives his reader tantalizing hints of the kinds of moral compromises that enabled Jay Gatsby to buy a mansion on the shore in West Egg, but our judgment of Gatsby is informed mostly by his apparent fragility and the single-mindedness of his passion.

Of all the American novelists, however, it was Theodore Dreiser who produced the most complete, ambitious, and complex portrait of an American business tycoon. In a series of three novels—*The Financier* (1912), *The Titan* (1914), and *The Stoic* (1931)—Dreiser created a portrait of a ruthless magnate, Frank Cowperwood, whose charm lies in his utter candor about his hunger for money and power and about his willingness to utilize unsavory means to secure them. With precision and with prescience, the trilogy illustrates just why Americans so often suspend judgment when considering the ethical lapses of corporate leaders.

Cowperwood makes his fortune first in banking in Philadelphia, then (after a stint in the penitentiary for fraud) in the dynamic natural gas and street railway industries in Chicago. Dreiser spares us no detail of the ruthless tactics that his protagonist uses to achieve his ends. Once he fixes on the streetcar business, Cowperwood announces early on that industry dominance is his goal, and he deliberately sows dissension among his competitors through a combination of misinformation, threats, and deception. When it serves his purposes, he participates with gusto in the corrupt world of Chicago politics, bribing generously, and cheerfully changing parties when the political winds shift. He manipulates the financial markets to serve his own ends, and he bends the law to his own advantage. In one memorable scene, a small businessman named Raymond Purdy tries to hold out for an above-market price for a useless warehouse on a piece of property vital to the development of one of Cowperwood's streetcar lines. One Saturday, a demolition crew shows up and the warehouse is destroyed. Mr. Purdy tries to pursue justice in the courts, but he is thwarted at every turn, and he receives nothing for his property. Cowperwood's project proceeds unimpaired, and Dreiser allows his reader to savor the sheer, heartless roguishness of his protagonist.[6] Cowperwood does not see himself as unethical. He is quite aware that some of his actions press at the boundaries of the lawful and the acceptable, but he sees himself as playing within a set of rules that he had no part in establishing.

The Cowperwood trilogy stands alongside many other novels, films, and other products of American culture that have helped Americans personalize the whole field of business ethics. Writers like Dreiser have both reflected American fascination with the titans, and have also helped to shape attitudes about them. Dreiser's portrait had its counterpart in the work of muckraking journalists of his day, who exposed the excesses of corporate America, while at the same time scarcely concealing the journalists' admiration for the raffish and outlandish character of the men whom they pilloried. Oscillating between outrage and admiration, we see business leaders in the context of a society built on conquest, so we both exaggerate their importance and suspend our judgment. It is, in the end, their "intent" that matters more than their actions, and there is no malfeasance in the intent to succeed.

The business scandals of the 1990s and the early part of the twenty-first century have tested and extended the American focus on the titans of business. A decade of controversy regarding the Microsoft Corporation has focused on the figure of Bill Gates, a new breed of titan who is nevertheless widely admired and vilified in much the same terms as the titans of Frank Cowperwood's era. Microsoft's hunger for dominance is seen as an extension of Gates the man. The scandals at Enron, WorldCom, and Tyco, among others, are often portrayed as extensions of the misdeeds of a handful of individuals at the top of the corporate pyramid, and the new form of narrative for relating their stories is the widely publicized trial.

Yet as the Tyco trial in 2003 and 2004 revealed, judgments about these corporate leaders can be complex. For six months, the prosecution of Dennis Koslowski and other leaders of the Tyco Corporation laid out a careful documentation of the ways in which the executives had systematically siphoned off corporate funds for private use, thereby, in effect, robbing the company's assets and by extension its stockholders. Yet the case ended in a highly publicized mistrial, when the press reported that one juror, a seventy-nine year-old woman named Ruth Jordan, was holding out against conviction. As Jordan reported publicly once the trial was over, she was fully persuaded that the Koslowski and his associates had raided the till at Tyco. But she was not persuaded that they had actually *intended* to commit a crime. By Jordan's lights, they were simply doing what was expected, cooperating at every stage with Tyco's board of directors, and acting in a way consistent with business practice across the country. Without intent, where was the crime?[7]

The American emphasis on the character of the leaders of business enterprise suggests the enormous importance of leadership in developing corporate ethics programs. One response has been to focus attention on penalties for senior executives who abuse their position. Removing "bad apples," instituting harsh punishments for white-collar criminals, spreading around accountability: These are some of the remedies that emerge in response to this strand of thinking. At the same time, it has become a truism in the field that no program of any depth or impact can take root without a CEO of the highest integrity, and one who is willing to make the program a public priority. This emphasis suggests, in effect, that one of the most important steps a corporation can take with regard to ethics is to find leaders of impeccable character.

Yet history suggests that this ideal of the CEO as moral beacon may be an unreliable foundation for improved corporate behavior. For one thing, some CEOs' conception of righteousness may not extend broadly enough to satisfy a full set of expectations: Andrew Carnegie and John D. Rockefeller saw their profits as instruments of godliness, made possible by business decisions regarding labor management and competitive practices that others saw as crass exploitation. For another thing, the pressures on corporate leaders from both inside and outside their enterprises to present themselves as models of dynamism and innovation come into inevitable conflict with standards of ethics. American ambivalence about power, as reflected in Dreiser's trilogy and the Tyco trial, tends to reinforce the moral authority of leadership itself, tempting those in power to consider the health of their company as a public good. Furthermore, as circumstances change, so do the standards of ethical behavior, and leaders schooled in one era may find their ideals out of step with the expectations of another age. These trends suggest that while ethics programs may indeed have to start with strong leadership, they need also to make leaders themselves a principal focus of their activities.

Business Conduct

Analyzing the ethics of business is a quite different matter if our gaze is focused on corporations as entities, rather than on the character of the individual men and women who lead them. We may be considering the very same types of competitive skullduggery and abuses of power, but their causes and consequences look quite different if our working assumption is that corporate entities have a collective life and character. In this perspective, we see corporations in their broader context, as members of particular industries and as part of American business culture. It challenges the widespread myth that for-profit organizations are inherently amoral enterprises, capable only of focusing collectively on profit and survival; it assumes that the actions of corporations as entities can be weighed in moral terms, and that those both inside and outside the organization can influence a corporation to change its behavior according to ethical standards.

This strand of thinking about the ethics of American business could only begin to take hold in the middle of the nineteenth century, once the industrial revolution gave birth to larger corporate entities. Before that era, the scale of business was smaller, the character of business culture more personal, and it was quite natural to think of business ethics purely in terms of the character of the rich. In an era of dynamic change, however, the corporation itself came to have a public face. With technology and transportation driving the scale and scope of commerce, the standards of business behavior were in a state of flux. Decision making was by necessity decentralized in larger companies, so the source of corporate actions became harder to trace. The nineteenth century gave birth to powerful new symbols of the faceless corporation: first the railroads, with their vivid marking of the American landscape; then the more abstract concept of the trusts in steel and oil, conjuring up images of secret power and manipulation.

Looking at corporations rather than at individuals calls our attention to particular corporate tactics, rather than to individual expressions of unbridled rapacity. Nineteenth-century companies found ingenious ways to press legal and ethical boundaries in their pursuit of advantage and profit. The notion of "conflict of interest," for example, took some time to develop. In the middle of the nineteenth century, it was commonplace for directors of railroads to organize, as a side business, construction companies with a specialty in building railroad tracks. The railroad company, then, would outsource its line construction business to these new companies, thereby allowing its own directors to negotiate with themselves and profit personally by the arrangements. These types of insider deals applied to the purchase of materials and supplies in the railroad industry, as well as in other fields.[8]

Insider deals that benefited individuals were comparatively simple to spot and criticize, but the more complicated relations between corporations gave rise to a realm of business ethics that was more difficult to assess. One such area was "restraint of trade," the arrangements between powerful corporations that protected the mutual interests of large players. Concerned that chaotic competition would lead to price wars that would undermine the stability of their industries, corporations worked together to form "pools" through which competitors agreed on prices for particular products and services. Successful pools, which were legal at the beginning of this era, protected the profits of corporations, although it was notoriously difficult to enforce discipline through such loose and informal arrangements. Sometimes pools were formed within single industries; sometimes they involved arrangements between complementary industries, such as between railroads and shipping companies.

It was by no means straightforward, however, to assess restraint of trade practices in ethical terms. "Pooling" struck many outsiders as a gross violation of standards of fairness, since the practice kept prices artificially high at the expense of other businesses and ultimately the consumer. But to other observers, the benefits of providing stability and predictability in the system outweighed its disadvantages. After all, cutthroat competition had its own set of negative consequences: the temptation to cut costs by sacrificing quality and even cheating the buyer; driving honest brokers from the marketplace; and the creation of a boom-and-bust cycle that made it difficult for consumers to plan ahead with regard to services and costs. It was easy to inveigh against pooling in abstract moral terms, but the issue was more complicated in light of the overall state of American business and society. Historians looking back on this period have disagreed about who was more virtuous: the corporate leader who supported a pool that created stability, or the courageous individual who broke the agreement and helped undo a form of monopoly.[9] In the era after the Civil War, some pools developed into more comprehensive forms of "trusts," which allowed an ever smaller number of companies to control costs and prices more thoroughly.

Contemporary controversies over practices in financial reporting, accounting, and company value have their historical antecedents in the nineteenth century as well. Financial reporting, even to company insiders, was virtually nonexistent at the beginning of the industrial era.

The absence of complete or even partial financial reports allowed corporations to operate with relative impunity, and it put buyers and sellers of their stock at an enormous disadvantage. Public pressure in the form of media attention and legislation gradually brought about more complete disclosure by the beginning of the twentieth century, but it was still very difficult for the public to trace or even to understand the precise nature of complex corporate transactions.

At the beginning of the industrial era, American corporations had a comparatively free hand with regard to these business practices, but by the early years of the twentieth century, a regulatory environment began to curb corporate excesses. Landmark federal legislation like the Interstate Commerce Act (1887) and the Sherman Anti-Trust Act (1890) embodied the new focus on business practice by addressing corporate behavior on a large scale, and by attempting to create a public counterweight to the concentration of power and influence in the private sector. While vigorous enforcement of legislation was uneven (it took two decades for the Sherman Anti-Trust Act to come fully to fruition, with the breakup of Standard Oil in 1912), one question was settled definitively by the early years of the twentieth century: There was no longer any dispute over the idea that the behavior of corporations toward their stakeholders and toward one another was a matter of public concern.

Beginning around 1910, American industries also began to police themselves through the development of the first codes of ethics. These codes developed first in trade associations, especially in industries comprised of many small businesses, as opposed to major industries dominated by corporate giants. Smaller concerns, after all, had more to gain than large companies from informal agreements that restrained predatory practices. Hence, pioneers in developing codes of ethics included such groups as the National Ice Cream Manufacturers' Association, the National Hay Association, the National Knitted Outerwear Association, the National Bottle Manufacturers' Association, and the Memorial Craftsmen of America. The codes attempted to restrain unfair competition by condemning underpricing, deceptive advertising, bribery, incomplete public reporting, and underhanded efforts to steal away customers from competitors. These agreements were voluntary and entirely unenforceable, except through the threat of expulsion from the association, but they served as a check on commercial anarchy. "In the relations between competitors," wrote an optimistic early student of these codes,

> we see the emergence of a great ethical principle. It is generally called Co-operation. I am more inclined to speak of it as the Principle of Common Interest. When men in the same line of trade recognize that they have a common interest and act accordingly, with due regard for the rights of the public, their relations become to that extent more normal, harmonious, productive. . . . Following the principle of common interest is proving a better way of doing business than the old method of pursuing merely individual advantage.[10]

Codes were no guarantee of actual ethical behavior, but they were an indication of the increasing acceptance by industry itself of a company-centered view of business ethics. It is also important that these earlier initiatives took root in industry consortia, enabling companies to adopt ethical standards while minimizing the risk of competitive disadvantage. Developing ethics programs through consortia may, in fact, be a very practical way to achieve progress, but it also suggests the difficulty of counting on improvement in the absence of agreement among peers.

Considering corporate practice in the context of individual industries became a standard feature of the American landscape over the course of the twentieth century, and the source of considerable public and government attention. Major scandals rippled across the country with regularity, in widely different industries. In 1905, the focus was on the practices of major life insurance companies, which had conspired to drive smaller competitors from the field.[11] In the early 1960s, the electrical industry, led by General Electric and Westinghouse, was under the microscope for its schemes of bid rigging and price fixing.[12] Bribery around the world was the center of attention in the 1970s, with international players in defense and oil in the hot seat.

For our purposes, what is most important here is that a view of business ethics in terms of corporate and industry behavior has become a fixture. This view coexists with, and does not replace, the older strand of thinking that focuses on the substantive and symbolic actions of individuals. A focus on business practice concentrates attention on a corporation's behavior as part of its peer community. Does it engage in anticompetitive practices? Does it seek unfair advantage through immoral arrangements with suppliers or public officials? Does it adhere to the regulations of industry as promulgated by federal and state governments? Do its financial reporting processes adequately inform its investors? It is true that improvement of the standards of business practices not only benefits the industry but ultimately benefits the larger public as well. But the limitation of this perspective is that it is prone to narrow its scope of inquiry, and to be generous in comparing one corporation's behavior to those of its competitors. The focus on business conduct has led to productive oversight and self-regulation of American industry, but it can also serve to deflect attention away from the impact of business on the widest dimensions of American politics and society.

Putting Workers First

Labor relations are not always discussed in terms of business ethics, but workers are a key "stakeholder" in any consideration of corporate behavior. When considering the actions of tycoons or the business conduct of corporate entities, the treatment of employees is an important topic, but it tends to play a relatively minor role in ethical assessments. In the early codes of ethics, for example, fair and safe working conditions are mentioned nearly universally, but these clauses tend to be minor entries on a long list of topics.[13] Yet for many observers, the treatment of workers has been the starting point for judging corporate behavior, rather than merely an entry on a comprehensive list. With this consideration paramount, a different set of issues takes center stage: working conditions and questions of safety; employment practices, including discrimination; the labor of children and other disadvantaged populations; fair procedures in matters of discipline, promotion, and termination; the rights of workers to organize, and the responses of corporations to labor unions. Labor issues are not always thought of as matters of ethics per se. But to those for whom labor comes first, an ethics initiative that sidesteps this question can never be legitimate or complete.

Most often, the focus has been on exploitation. Starting early in the industrial era, the incidence of death and injury led to outcries about unsafe working conditions. The rise of labor unions in the years after the Civil War led to a series of bitter battles with American industry; among the most notable were the violent strike-breaking tactics in the steel industry in the 1890s, overseen close up by Henry Frick and implicitly endorsed from a safe distance by Andrew Carnegie.[14] During the Progressive Era, the photographs of Lewis Hine alerted Americans to the prevalence and social costs of child labor, a practice eventually curtailed (although not ended) through legislation. Discriminatory practices of businesses with respect to women and minority employees were exposed and to some extent corrected over the course of the twentieth century. In the era of globalization, the assessment of corporate performance in this area has been carried around the globe, with attention to the labor practices of multinational corporations in their facilities in the developing world. Each of these familiar aspects of the history of business and labor has its own set of narratives and debates.

What is important for our purposes is that these issues represent the single most significant standard of business ethics for a substantial segment of the American public. Does an organization provide fair and adequate compensation for its workforce? Do fringe benefits adequately protect workers from major expenses in terms of health care and other forms of catastrophe? Is the working environment safe and healthy? Do workers have adequate protection from harassment and abuse from their superiors? Are employees sufficiently protected from arbitrary or abrupt dismissal from their jobs? Do workers have adequate opportunity to organize to lobby for rights and privileges that they feel that they deserve? Corporations prefer to recognize these as issues best dealt with by human resources departments. But even companies themselves have come to recognize that the treatment of employees is as much an ethics issue as conflict of interest or competitive practices. Since human resources departments are established principally to enact the policies and reflect the interests of management, they tend to be inadequate, by themselves, as ethics offices for labor relations. This suggests an area of vulnerability for corporations striving to become model citizens: the challenge of creating independent internal mechanisms that fairly serve the interests of the average worker.

Some Americans, however, have taken a very different approach to the ethics of labor practice. Rather than focusing on corporate exploitation, they have viewed American business as an opportunity for creating a community based on moral uplift. This idea of the corporation as moral community receives less attention than the standard portrait of exploitation, but it is worth our sustained attention, because many contemporary business ethics programs reflect and extend it.

From the earliest era of industrial development, some leaders believed that one of the most important functions of American business was to create an environment that would improve both the lives and the character of their workers. As the persuasive power of churches weakened, and as the growth of cities imperiled the ideal of close-knit, small-town communities, some began to look to the factory to halt the slide of virtue. Industrial facilities, after all, were where an increasing number of Americans spent most of their waking hours. Besides, workers were a captive audience.

The mills of Lowell, Massachusetts, provided one setting for this type of social experimentation. In the 1830s and 1840s, the mills employed young women from all over New England who left (primarily) rural homes and families in search both of economic opportunity and a modicum of independence. Housed on site in the shadow of the mills, these workers found themselves "protected" by a series of rules and programs intended both to assure their reliability as employees and to keep them on the path to righteousness. From the point of view of their employers, these programs used the corporate structure to effect positive social change through fortifying the character of a generation of otherwise lost young women. From the point of view of contemporary social critics and later historians, these programs represented a paternalistic form of social control: Released from the restrictive sphere of rural New England, the mill workers found themselves trapped in an equally oppressive environment that monitored their every movement.[15]

This conception of the corporation as a moral community did not fade away with nineteenth-century evangelicalism. Indeed, it received an enormous boost from the systematic social science of the Progressive Era. The first decades of the twentieth century gave birth to the development that was first called "welfare work" and eventually came to be called "welfare capitalism." American businesses, wearied and bloodied from labor strife, began to take a new tack, placing an emphasis on "human relations" and benefits programs that leaders hoped would create a sense of common interests among ownership, management, and the workers. One of the innovators in this field was Colorado Fuel and Iron (CF & I), owned by John Rockefeller, Jr. Rocked by violent labor struggles in the 1910s that culminated in the famous "Ludlow Massacre" in 1914, CF & I instituted the "Rockefeller Plan" in 1915. This initiative created a system of employee representation in company decision making, and committed the corporation to greater transparency in its wage scales, employment practices, and observance of the mining laws.[16] While the Rockefeller Plan never fully lived up to its promise of employee empowerment, it provided an important model for rethinking the relationship between labor and management, and for consideration of a company's obligations toward its workers as an essential element of business practice.

Ford Motor Company put into place an even more ambitious plan, which vividly illustrated the strengths and the drawbacks of the welfare capitalism ideology. The company was growing rapidly in the years after 1910, as it began to perfect its assembly-line techniques. But the assembly-line method gave birth to a significant labor problem. Efficiency depended on a reliable workforce; if an employee, trained to handle a specific task on the assembly line, did not stay on the job, or if his attendance was erratic, the gap at his station could disrupt the entire process. If a worker was drinking too much, or if illness or conflict at home interfered with the regularity of his habits, his attendance suffered. So Ford introduced a series of measures to help its workers stay on the straight and narrow: incentives for workers to save a portion of their earnings, a "Medical Department" to promote health, and a primitive ethics program to encourage workers to abandon bad habits. An in-house magazine, *Ford Times*, derided the spoiled and dissolute "dude employe" [sic], who wears a "high collar" and "is not the one that knuckles down to hard work. . . . The dude employe does not like perspiration, so he sees that he does not exert himself." The magazine listed a series of "profit chokers"—bad habits that cost the corporation money—which included "doctoring records to suit the boss" and "'padded' pay rolls through tardiness and shirking" and "employes working 'their' way instead of the Company's."[17]

Ford's efforts in this area reached their apogee with the introduction of the "Five Dollar Day" in 1914. This program offered a daily wage of nearly double the going rate to any worker who lived a clean and thrifty life and who was willing to undergo inspection of his private affairs by the Ford Sociological Department, which was established for this express purpose. To qualify, the company explained, a worker had to "show himself sober, steady, industrious, and [he] must satisfy the superintendent and staff that his money will not be wasted in riotous living." The wage was described as a "profit-sharing" plan; workers on the "Five Dollar Day" were encouraged to think of themselves as partners with management.

The Sociological Department proceeded to employ a battery of investigators, primarily recruited from the existing ranks of white-collar employees of the company. (Ford did not want to hire college-trained sociologists; the thinking was that their academic training rendered them unfit for dealing with real people in the real world.[18]) These investigators made scheduled and surprise home visits, both interviewing workers at home and checking up on what was happening with their families while workers were on the job. Ford was particularly obsessed with the virtue of "thrift": If a worker was saving money, the thinking went, then other virtues were likely to follow in its wake. Bank records, therefore, were among the investigators' primary sources of information. The incentive system was clear: Workers in compliance received compensation at substantially higher levels than those who fell out of grace with the Sociological Department.

Ford promoted the Five Dollar Day with a vigorous internal public relations campaign. It published "Human Interest Stories" that illustrated success (the alcoholic who gave up drink, and then, after the requisite time, earned his way to prosperity) and failure (the "Five Dollar Day" man who got married and started squandering his pay on household goods and later gambling and liquor, and who therefore lost his privileges under the program).[19] These publications touted not only the value of the program for Ford's workforce, but the value of the program for the workers themselves. Company profits, the character of individual workers, and the corporate sense of family were inextricably intertwined. The program was paternalistic and intrusive, but as its chronicler has pointed out, it also "marked a progressive shift from the older idea of individual and moral causes of poverty to the more modern idea of social and environmental ones."[20]

The advent of World War I heralded the decline and the eventual abandonment of the Five Dollar Day. The U.S. government took advantage of the structure of the Sociological Department to co-opt its investigations under the guise of national security in wartime. The program became a tool for cracking down on Michigan's immigrant population and for promoting patriotism in its crudest sense. The postwar recession of 1920–1921 proved its final undoing, as the program finally became a victim of cost-cutting measures.

Ford's early-twentieth-century efforts suggest that concern about developing a moral community among employees has long-standing roots. It also shows the hazards of this type of endeavor. Ford boasted of its program as good both for the workers (who ostensibly benefited by developing better personal habits) and for the company (which benefited by a more reliable workforce). But to critics of the time, and even more to later generations, the Five Dollar Day looks ominously like a full-fledged effort at oppressive social control. It raises the question of whether it is possible for corporations to undertake a self-conscious program of moral uplift without threatening cherished ideals of individuality and independence.

During the 1920s, however, welfare capitalism flourished, and to some extent corporations minimized the paternalism that had characterized Ford's efforts. Major companies like United States Steel, General Electric, and Procter & Gamble made visible public voluntary commitments to policies that extended benefits and privileges to their workforces. These commitments included, in various circumstances, pension, housing, medical and insurance plans, commitment to high wages, and the development of in-house structures for employee representation. The leaders of these corporations spoke openly about trying to instill a family atmosphere in a large corporation, in which all the members embraced a common mission and felt a common stake in the corporation's success.[21] Although the economic shock of the Great Depression took a severe toll on welfare capitalism, its elements persisted in a different form in the postwar era in such companies as Eastman Kodak and Sears Roebuck.[22]

Welfare capitalism was a study in mixed motives. It represented some personal convictions of American business leaders, who genuinely believed that they could achieve a harmony of interests within their corporations. Yet it was also in many cases a self-conscious effort to undermine worker radicalism through co-optation. Companies often provided just enough new benefits to stave off discontent, and they created in-house employee representation plans that could be controlled and monitored, unlike the traditional labor unions.

No American business would dare to intrude so openly into the lives of its workers in the twenty-first century as Ford Motor Company did in the 1910s. Yet the conception of corporate ethics as a composite of the personal character of a company's workforce is very much alive. An employee-centered vision of business ethics, whether it focuses on the exploitation of workers or on the improvement of their character, represents an important contrast to focusing on the character of business leaders or on corporate business conduct. It can call our attention to a more democratic idea of business ethics, by conferring importance on the role and the actions of the wage workers at the bottom of the employment pyramid, but it also highlights issues of social control. Welfare capitalism was an important forerunner of the contemporary business ethics movement, both as an admirable model and as a cautionary tale.

Social Responsibility

A fourth conception of business ethics puts the primary emphasis on a corporation's impact on the outside world. It treats a business first and foremost as an integral part of its society (and sometimes of the global community), and it considers the role that companies play in shaping the conditions of life for the people with whom it comes into contact. This view assumes that corporations do in fact wield considerable power and influence over the world that they inhabit, and it treats their impact as a set of deliberate decisions. It also assumes that public perceptions of corporations matter, that business ethics can be influenced from without, as well as take root from within.

Attention to the collateral impact of industry goes back to the dawn of the industrial era. Its most prevalent form for many years was an emerging environmentalism, a critique of the scarring impact of industry on the natural landscape. In Victorian England, the air blackened and the water fouled by a coal-burning industrial boom were manifestations and symbols of commercial callousness. In the United States, the railroad and the steam engine served as representations of a spreading industrial impulse that seemed to pay little attention to the human consequences of its march. These early critiques were, however, relatively general. They were aimed more at industry writ large, rather than at the actions of particular corporations. They were less about business ethics, with its concentration on decisions by corporations and their leaders, and more about a critique of the system of industrial capitalism.

A more specific view of what came to be known as corporate social responsibility began to emerge in a coherent way in the United States in the years after World War II. The triumph of free enterprise and the universal recognition of American influence on a global scale laid the groundwork for a perspective that generally endorsed capitalism but sought to humanize it by asking businesses to serve social ends. In the 1940s, for example, the Federal Council of Churches, the multidenominational organ of the American Protestant establishment, commissioned a series of books on ethics and economic life that touched on Christian perspectives but were intended to frame the issues in a secular and accessible manner. In the first of these volumes, published in 1953, Howard R. Bowen, a professor of economics at Williams College, developed a detailed conception of the social responsibilities of businessmen.

According to Bowen, the strength of American prosperity was making possible a new and more generous idea of the role of the corporation in society:

> The day of plunder, human exploitation, and financial chicanery by private businessmen has largely passed. And the day when profit maximization was the sole criterion of business success is rapidly fading. We are entering an era when private business will be judged solely in terms of its demonstrable contribution to the general welfare. Leading thinkers among businessmen understand this clearly. For them, therefore, the acceptance of obligations to workers, consumers, and the general public is a condition for survival of the free-enterprise system. Hence, even if the interests of stockholders be taken as the sole aim of business, concern for broader social objectives becomes obligatory for management.[23]

This optimistic assessment rests on a fundamental assumption that in the postwar era, American businesses can *afford* to care about their impact on the general welfare. Accordingly, Bowen lists a series of social goods to which he believes businesses should be contributing, and against which they should be judged. These include the broad distribution of a high standard of living; a widespread sense of economic progress and security; abstract concepts like order, justice, and freedom; and "the development of the individual person." The traditional concern about the natural environment is, in this scheme, just one area among many that fall within the responsibility of businessmen and the corporations that they lead.

What is going to drive businessmen to show the concern for the general welfare that Bowen believes is necessary (and perhaps inevitable)? Bowen places a great deal of weight on "informal social controls." Corporate leaders, he points out, are part of peer networks, and their social standing within those networks matters a great deal to them. Public pressure for corporations to act positively has a huge impact on these leaders. "The means of achieving higher morality in business behavior," Bowen argues, "is to create public attitudes that enlarge the moral responsibilities of business. Once this is done, business, with its new and broadened concern for public approval, will respond."[24] Ultimately, he suggests, one of the most decisive factors in encouraging corporate responsibility will be the egos of their leaders. Businessmen want to be loved, and they enjoy the role of educating and leading the broader public. Once they understand that they can play this part only by making their organizations into good corporate citizens, positive results will naturally follow.[25]

Bowen's analysis may seem unduly sanguine about the prospects for corporate concern for the broader community, but his basic premises undergird what has become a broadly accepted principle in twenty-first-century corporate America. Corporate social responsibility has become so fashionable that its acronym (CSR) can stand alone, and the concept has become a tool by which companies have attempted to turn a public relations problem into a public relations asset. Rather than passively allowing others to form judgments on their harmful impact on local and national communities, corporations have called attention to specific actions that they have taken to improve people's lives. Bowen's emphasis on the importance of public relations in encouraging these efforts was prescient: CSR programs now form the backbone of many of corporate America's largest advertising campaigns, especially in industries (big tobacco comes to mind) that have been vulnerable to public criticism for their social impact.

Contemporary advertising campaigns like those of Philip Morris follow a long-standing tradition of humanizing American industry through the mass media. Roland Marchand has traced this effort to define an image of a "corporate soul," beginning most dramatically with the thirty-year campaign launched by AT&T in 1908 to convince American consumers that a big, warm-hearted monopoly was exactly what the United States needed in the telecommunications industry. AT&T drew on nostalgia for small-town life, sentimental ideas about the average working man and working woman, the pull of patriotism, and the lure of bigness itself to try to convince the public that big business, far from being heartless, had a core mission to touch and improve the lives of people across the country. "Ma Bell" trumpeted the ideal of "service" in the figure of a "storm-swept" employee repairing a phone line, or the operator acting as a "weaver of speech." Other companies promoted their progressive policies toward their workers, or their contributions to the unemployed during the Great Depression. Marchand credits these campaigns with successfully deflecting widespread public criticism of monopolistic practices and aggressive profit seeking in the first half of the twentieth century.[26]

This is not to say that corporate social responsibility is merely a public relations ploy. American corporations spend tens of millions of dollars annually on community improvement programs in areas like education, youth development, beautification, health, and social services to the needy. In an era of reduced government services, these programs are significant contributions to private-sector philanthropy. Promoters of CSR argue that these programs represent corporate ethics at its best. If a business is going to be judged by its impact on individual lives, what better way to assess its values than by looking at the positive steps it takes to ameliorate the communities in which it conducts its business?

Corporate critics have responded by calling attention to different types of community impact. Environmental issues remain near the top of the list of concerns, but that list is much longer than it was in the early years of industrialization. Community impact has expanded to include the nature of the products that a business produces, the economic impact of a company on consumers, and the side effects of its research and development activities. The new wrinkle in the twenty-first century is the increasing emphasis on global impact in an era of multinational businesses. Emerging issues include child labor practices in Asia, industry effects on global warming, and corporate intrusion in domestic politics in developing countries. Critics agree with CSR supporters that community impact is the first standard of measuring business ethics, but they draw very different conclusions about how well corporations meet that standard.

The Perils of Profits

A fifth strand of thought about business ethics focuses on the nature of capitalism itself. As we have seen in the example of Robert Keayne, mistrust about profit seeking has its roots in the earliest moments of American history. A small but persistent minority has voiced a deep-seated strain of skepticism about the corrupting power of free enterprise over the past 300 years. These critics do not look at corporate misdeeds as simply the actions of greedy individuals, nor as aberrations from a healthy norm, nor as accidents of mismanagement or negligence. Instead, they see corporate foul play as the inevitable result of a system that encourages aggressive competition, rewards the ambitious and the cold-hearted, and makes prosperity for the few a greater social good than the well-being of the many. In this view, corporate ethics efforts are a distraction, a gloss over inevitable problems of exploitation and corruption.

At times, this strand has taken the form of socialism and other, more radical forms of political thought. Some of America's most incisive thinkers and writers have weighed in as skeptics about the premises of capitalism, from the agrarian outlook of Thomas Jefferson, to the "single tax" system of Henry George, to the horrifying portrayal of meat factories in Upton Sinclair's *The Jungle,* to the numerous critics who decried the failures of capitalism amid the widespread suffering of the Great Depression. The cadences of the argument are familiar in our own time, in rhetorical attacks on the military–industrial complex and on multinational corporations. Taken far enough, these critiques are so comprehensive that they offer little common ground for discussion with those concerned about corporate ethics.

For our purpose, however, I want to explore a less radical version of the same skepticism that is shared by a wider swath of the American public. Despite a prevailing laissez-faire ideology, Americans have seldom viewed the pursuit of profit as an inalienable right, and they have often shown concern about the corrupting nature of profit itself, when pursued in particular circumstances. One such circumstance has been the mix of business and war. The United States has always relied on private industry to supply the military needs of the nation, but Americans have been deeply ambivalent about profits earned in wartime, or even on defense in times of peace. This variation on a more general skepticism about free enterprise has obvious relevance when considering the corporate ethics of the defense industry in our own time.

Concern about war profits began during the Colonial and Revolutionary eras, a time when frontier wars kept demand for supplies high, when price gouging in times of emergency was rampant, and when plunder and looting were routine sources of income for professional soldiers. As essential as supplies were to the maintenance of European settlements and later to the successful war of independence, a natural stigma attached to the merchants who made these military efforts possible. During the Revolutionary War, the colonists' reliance on the rhetoric of "virtue" brought down criticism on patriots like the New Jersey merchant Robert Morris, who became, somewhat unfairly, a living symbol of exploitation of military funds.[27]

Widespread public outrage about war profits accelerated during the Civil War. In a notorious early incident, Brooks Brothers, the New York clothier, sold low-quality uniforms for the New York volunteers who enlisted in the Union Army. The ragged appearance of these troops spurred public wrath at what became known as the "shoddyocracy," the legion of suppliers accused of providing inferior products to the Union military effort. Other major U.S. companies received a jump start from war expenditures; American Express, for example, thrived on the burgeoning railroad express business, sending packages from family and friends to soldiers in the field, and making a tidy profit by shipping corpses home from the front. The Civil War also created the country's first weapons millionaire, firearms manufacturer Samuel Colt. As the war dragged on over four long years, public outrage mounted at the figure that the *New York Times* called "the self-styled loyalist, who puts money in his purse at the expense of soldiers who go to fight rebels." [28]

By the time of World War I, concerns about profits in wartime were no longer exclusively the province of editorialists: They had become the stuff of legislation. As war began in Europe in 1914 and 1915, public attention focused on major concerns like Du Pont, whose chemical products included various powders used in new forms of weaponry. A major supplier to the Allies, Du Pont had made so much money in the military powder business by 1916 that, even before U.S. entry into the war, Congress passed the first excess profits tax in American history, aimed specifically at the company's wartime gains. Critics of big business began not only to question the idea of windfall war profits, but also to accuse industry of fomenting conflict for the sake of financial returns. When Congressman John Nelson blamed the war itself on "Big Business, The Interests, the System, the Corporations, the Money Power, Wall Street, or the Rockefellers and the Morgans," he was near the front of a long line of mainstream Americans who have not hesitated to name the profit motive as the prime mover in U.S. defense policy.

This line of argument reached an apex in 1934 and 1935, when Congressman Gerald P. Nye of North Dakota and Congressman Arthur H. Vandenberg of Michigan presided over a set of hearings that historian Stuart Brandes calls "the most sweeping consideration of the war profits issue in American history." The Nye-Vandenberg committee took as its ostensible field of inquiry American participation in the Great War, but its impact was felt during a time when conflicts in Europe were heating up and American industry was positioning itself for a share of the defense business that might result. The committee and its staff waged an unabashed assault on the industry practices of two decades before, focusing on excess profits, insider deals, and complex financial transactions. It implicitly advanced the argument that "merchants of death" had dominated United States policy during World War I, and that they were lurking still, waiting for their opportunity to exploit death and destruction again. The committee's conclusions have not stood the test of time well; historians have faulted its partisan character and even compared its tactics to the later McCarthy-era hearings. In its own day, however, the committee was a powerful driver of public opinion; a Gallup poll conducted in 1937 found that 82 percent of the American people favored the prohibition of the sale of munitions by private parties.[29]

Some of the most egregious profit making in the war industry was curbed by federal legislation during the first half of the twentieth century. Nevertheless, the powerful skepticism about the mix of profits and war continued to play a powerful part in the years after World War II, reaching a crescendo in the critique of an unholy alliance between government and business during the Vietnam War. American skepticism about defense industry profits has not just been the province of a radical fringe—it forms a minor but deeply ingrained part of mainstream thinking. As such, it stands for a view of business ethics that questions the premise of the essentially virtuous role of free enterprise. It fuels assumptions about the immorality of war profits that make it difficult to apply conventional ideas of business ethics to the defense industry. To those who start from this perspective, ethics in the defense industry will always begin with a substantial handicap.

These perspectives represent five distinct starting points for considering ethics in American business: the role of the corporate leader; the conduct of businesses according to industry practice; the experience of the average worker; the impact on the larger community; and the nature of profit itself. They do not represent a common consensus on the behavior of corporations, or a consistency of ideas across time and geography. To the contrary, they suggest the very great challenge that corporations face when creating ethics programs, precisely because the true scope of the field is so broad. These strands of thought are less contrasting viewpoints than they are shades of emphasis, but they lead in very different directions and to very different judgments. Because of their deep historical roots, they also have a profound influence on the way that contemporary Americans think about corporate players, and they shape the thinking of scholars and practitioners in the ethics field.

Critics of corporations, as well as their defenders, tend to begin with one of these perspectives and stick with it. While this can lead to trenchant critiques and seamless defenses, it often creates discussions at cross-purposes. A company is hailed as a leader of corporate ethics for its work in an American neighborhood, while decried as a global villain for its labor practices overseas. Another trumpets its freedom from accounting scandals, while corporate watchdogs decry its chief executive for padding his own paycheck. Partisans of these perspectives might as well be speaking different languages.

The very breadth of these considerations suggests a daunting task for corporations. By its very nature, corporate ethics is an evolving process. In a world of rapidly changing standards and circumstances, no corporation can hope to operate with perfect integrity, especially under such a broad spectrum of expectations for busineses. Americans are uncommonly generous about failure, but only in the context of whole-hearted effort. Patching up a single problem will likely satisfy no one in the long run, when problems emerge in new and unforeseen areas. But this is just another way of saying that corporate ethics is a continuous process, rather than the rollout of a single product. What the history suggests is that responding to discrete problems of corruption or exploitation is a short-term fix. The challenge is to develop an approach that is sufficiently supple, dynamic, and self-critical to engage ethics issues in their most fundamental—and therefore most threatening—dimension.

chapter two

Success and Scandal

LOCKHEED MARTIN CORPORATION is the size of a small city, but its reach is global. Its 130,000 employees work in nearly 1000 facilities scattered around forty-five states and dozens of foreign countries. Each year in the twenty-first century, the corporation has sold more than $25 billion worth of airplanes, missiles, detection systems, information platforms, launchers, surveillance devices, and a host of services to support and maintain all of this equipment. During the 2003 Iraq War, 426 Lockheed Martin airplanes flew thousands of sorties, four different Lockheed Martin "smart weapons" were among the 20,000 guided missiles launched during combat operations, and these were just the beginning of the corporation's equipment and services put to use during the conflict. In early 2004, in the wake of the September 11, 2001, terrorist attacks and the Iraq War, the corporation had a backlog of more than $70 billion of equipment and services on order, the vast majority of it for the Department of Defense and other agencies of the U.S. government. Although a single corporate entity (LMT on the New York Stock Exchange), Lockheed Martin consists of more than two dozen "heritage companies": units, divisions, and even whole corporations that have become part of the Lockheed Martin family through merger and acquisition. It is a hulk of a company, spread liberally across the landscape, a producer of some of the world's most sophisticated, deadly, and speedy technology.

Yet as large as its shadow looms today, the corporation's self-image is of a much nimbler creature. The Lockheed name is associated with the first unlikely human experiments with flight in the first years of the twentieth century. Nearly a century later, the corporation still likes to think of itself as a pioneer at the cutting edge of human knowledge and exploration, a risk taker, an adventurer, a hothouse of innovation and independent thinking. A devil-may-care spirit lives, of course, in tension with the demands and bureaucracy of a Fortune 100 company, a tension that has profound implications for the nature of the company culture.

The scandals that led, eventually, to the development of Lockheed's ethics program began to take shape during the period when the company was making its transition from one of dozens of scrappy builders of airplanes into a bulwark of the U.S. defense establishment. The productiveness of the company's engineering culture depended on a hard-driving spirit of experimentation, a willingness to live outside the boundaries of the conventional, and a confidence in eventual success even in the face of initial evidence to the contrary. That spirit of pluck—some might call it hubris—made Lockheed a success where most others failed. It also helped to create a zealousness about the company's cause that made it easy to put the company's best interests before fussy standards of business conduct. Lockheed grew too important—and too self-important—to fail.

Taking Flight

Before the "merger of equals" with Martin Marietta, before the acquisition of the mile-long hangar in Fort Worth where General Dynamics built the F-16 fighter planes, before biting off pieces of Loral and IBM and General Electric, even before the space and missile divisions, there was the Loughead Aircraft Manufacturing Company, established in a small warehouse in Santa Barbara, California. The company was founded by two brothers, Allan and Malcolm Loughead, who were among the legions of young American men tinkering with the mechanics of speed and flight. Born to a hardy mother who had survived the departure of the boys' father by working as a journalist and a miner, the Loughead brothers grew up and made their way in California working on and selling bicycles, automobiles, and anything else that moved. Flying was a natural extension of their mechanical gifts; the brothers built their first airplane in 1913 and coaxed it into the air over San Francisco Bay on a sunny June day, where it circled over Alcatraz and Sausalito at a top speed of 63 miles an hour before returning safely to land.[1]

The fledgling company's fortunes ebbed and flowed over the next two decades, as it took different shapes and tried to establish its niche in an emerging industry. The Loughead brothers virtually handcrafted their first wooden planes in southern California, making their first sales to wealthy hobbyists, and, ironically, developing a model suitable for military use too late for deployment in World War I. Malcolm Loughead, discouraged by the company's prospects, left to pursue a plan to develop four-wheel hydraulic brakes for automobiles, so Allan Loughead persisted alone. The original company failed in the mid-1920s, but Allan found enough new investors to begin again. The new venture needed a new name, and since investors and customers alike had stumbled on the pronunciation of the original, the entity born in 1926 was christened the Lockheed Aircraft Company, with headquarters in what was then the sleepy Los Angeles suburb of Burbank.

The new company quickly developed its first major success—an aircraft that established the Lockheed name as a leader in the field, and brought fame and glamour—if not exactly fortune—to its founder. The plane was called the Vega, a four-passenger wooden monoplane. It was a Lockheed Vega that made the first nonstop transcontinental flight across the United States in 1928 (it took nineteen hours). A Vega made the first exploratory flight over the Antarctic, and set speed records for flights across the country and around the world. Amelia Earhart flew a Vega from Honolulu to Oakland, and Wiley Post's Vega set an unofficial altitude record of 55,000 feet. It was also in a Vega that Earhart plunged into the Pacific and Post crashed in the wilds of Alaska, taking humorist Will Rogers down with him.

Lockheed made headlines with the Vega, but then, as now, success made the company vulnerable to takeover. Having grown up as the extension of one engineer's ebullient personality, the company was acquired in 1929 by a new and faceless entity, the Detroit Aircraft Corporation, which aspired to be a General Motors of the air. Allan Lockheed was roughly pushed aside; the company he had founded was now no more than a profitable division of a conglomerate. The division continued to turn out successful products in its Burbank warehouse, but the spirit of innovation and adventure was distinctly under siege.

As it turned out, the Great Depression liberated Lockheed, and gave birth to the company in its modern, dynamic form. The Detroit Aircraft Corporation's vision of industry dominance plummeted along with the stock market; in the midst of the company's woes, the Lockheed division came up for sale. In 1932, it was purchased for $40,000 by a young businessman from Newton, Massachusetts, named Robert Ellsworth Gross. Gross was neither an engineer nor a pilot, but he had an instinct for the market. For the next three decades, he presided over the reborn Lockheed Aircraft Company and made it a leader of the industry.

In the 1910s, the Loughead brothers had built their first model planes with the assistance of a few engineers and a few dozen mechanics. When Robert Gross officially became chairman of the new Lockheed in 1934, the company had 300 employees. By 1938, when the company had developed its successful 10-seat Electra model, there were nearly 3,000 employees scurrying around the Burbank operation. That tenfold growth was only the beginning, for the Lockheed Aircraft Company became one of the prime beneficiaries of the second world war. In the late 1930s, the company became for the first time a serious provider of military aircraft. It developed the P-38 (Lightning), a twin-engine, twin-boom metal plane that the company first sold to Britain's Royal Air Force, which then became a mainstay of the full Allied war effort. By 1940, even before the United States had entered the war, there were 17,000 employees in Burbank. By 1943, when production reached its zenith, the company had swollen to 91,000 employees; production was so intensive and space so cramped that the manufacturing operations spilled outside the hangars, and planes in various stages of completion dotted the landscape. In 1944, Lockheed delivered more than 4,000 planes for use in the European and Asian theaters.

The war effort spurred production, and it also demanded innovation. It was not enough to build planes to transport personnel or to drop bombs; the U.S. Army Air Corps needed a jet fighter that could outfly and outperform the enemy aircraft. Responding to the need, Robert Gross set up a quasi-independent, top-secret research outfit in one corner of the Burbank operation. He gave control of the operation to a brilliant young University of Michigan graduate named Clarence Johnson, a man whom everyone knew as "Kelly." Kelly Johnson gathered around him the best and the brightest of Lockheed's engineering corps, and he turned them loose in a generative environment that was a peculiar combination of freewheeling experimentation and obsessive secrecy. In the absurdly short period of eight months, Johnson's team produced the XP-80, the Shooting Star, the first American jet fighter.

Johnson's operation was officially called the Lockheed Advanced Research and Development Program, but the bureaucratic name was a mismatch for the self-image of the team. The engineers thought of themselves as living on the edge, pushing the boundaries of traditional ideas, operating in an atmosphere of raffish rebelliousness, outside the public eye and even beyond the limits of discussion with family and friends. They adopted as the informal symbol of their unit the secret distillery in the woods made famous in Al Capp's popular "Li'l Abner." The cutting edge of Lockheed's aeronautics operation became known as the "Skunk Works."

The Skunk Works became the living symbol of Lockheed's quest for technological superiority. In the postwar years, the outfit developed a series of aircraft that made profits and headlines, most dramatically when the operation produced the U-2 spy plane, which (for a time) allowed low-risk, high-altitude flights to survey the military capacity of the Soviet Union. Equally notorious was Johnson's hard-driving, take-no-prisoners style, which earned him the fanatical loyalty of top engineers, but which also alienated some key constituencies, especially among Lockheed's customers in the U.S. Air Force and elsewhere. Zealous righteousness and intellectual arrogance produced results for the Skunk Works and for Lockheed; these traits also became badges of pride in a company that was now asserting its place as an essential defender of the American way and global freedom.

Lockheed had scaled down its capacity once the demand of the war years was past. By 1946 its employment level was at the prewar figure of 17,000. But its war success had put the company into position to become a major player in the military buildup of the Cold War era. Under the continuing leadership of Robert Gross and his brother Courtland, Lockheed expanded not only its operations but also its mission in the 1950s and 1960s Outgrowing the capacity of its Burbank headquarters, Lockheed opened a second facility for manufacturing aircraft in Marietta, Georgia, in 1951. In Marietta, Lockheed began building the C-130 cargo jet, the Hercules, one of the all-time aeronautics best-sellers, still very much in use and in production (in advanced forms) in the early years of the twenty-first century. The Lockheed Missiles and Space company opened its doors in Sunnyvale, California, the same year, building on the Skunk Works model to create an array of top-secret weapons products. Profits in the space and missile division would remain steady even when other parts of the corporation were floundering.

Bigger companies and bigger projects brought higher stakes, and Lockheed found itself locked in fierce competition with other new giants: Boeing, Northrop, MacDonnell, and a host of other pretenders that had committed themselves to vast operations requiring a constant infusion of new contracts to stay afloat. The prodigious cost of the research and development operations made failure unusually destructive. Moreover, the increasing dependence on business from the United States and other governments made the company subject to—and sometimes a shaper of—the vagaries of domestic and international politics.

Growth created huge opportunities for Lockheed, but also made the corporation vulnerable. Even after the temporary wartime employees went home, the corporation had a larger base of operations to maintain, and an imperative for expansion on a new scale. Its chief executive officer (CEO) was now a national figure, gracing the cover of *Time* in 1946, and beginning to serve as the personification of Lockheed's identity. A larger corporate entity created competition for resources and attention within the organization, making it tempting for executives and managers to seek an edge in business practice. A growing employee base meant more opportunities for labor problems, as the post-war boom raised worker expectations. Success made the corporation more accountable to an expanded sense of business ethics that was beginning to take hold. The combination of brashness and bigness made Lockheed a major player in American business, but it also brought the company to the brink of self-destruction.

The Grease Machine

Flying under the flag of the United Nations, American pilots dominated the skies during the Korean War at the beginning of the 1950s. But when Kelly Johnson traveled to Korea to talk with pilots about the performance of their fighter jets, he found a sea of discontent. The U.S. pilots told him that their skills were better than their Communist counterparts, but that the North Koreans were flying a better airplane, the Soviet-made MiG-15. Johnson came back home with a message for Lockheed and the Defense Department: Build us a faster, lighter, more maneuverable aircraft.

So Johnson's team got to work, and Lockheed produced a new jet fighter with exactly these characteristics. The company invested huge resources of time and money into a prototype that promised to be the follow-up to the XP-80, which had been produced so rapidly during World War II. The F-104, the Starfighter, made its debut in February 1954, but there were difficulties from the start. Johnson's design was ingenious, but it cut corners on nearly every element of the aircraft in order to maximize quickness. The design could only support a light and inadequate radar sight system; complex electronics were necessary to keep the aircraft stable, and, since pressurizing equipment had been jettisoned in order to save on weight, pilots had to wear uncomfortable space suits. A series of technical problems besieged the first test flights of the Starfighter; it took four years for the plane to come officially into service, and even then, the aircraft was almost immediately grounded for three months in order to fit a new engine.

Furthermore, it responded to a set of circumstances—those of the Korean War—that were already fading into the mists of time. By the mid-1950s, the U.S. Air Force was preoccupied with acquiring all-purpose aircraft that could take full advantage of advances in radar and other forms of technology to carry out a variety of different missions. The Starfighter was extraordinarily fast—it set a number of speed records over 1,000 miles per hour—but it was far from versatile. Lockheed had hoped to sell 2,500 Starfighters; the U.S. Air Force initially bought only 170.

Eager to recoup its investment and preserve jobs and profits, Lockheed turned to new markets. Its engineers frantically redesigned the Starfighter to enable it to carry the up-to-date equipment, and its salesmen began offering the plane wherever they could: on the overseas market. All around the world, countries were looking to replace their aging World War II aircraft. These nations included not only America's allies, but also its former adversaries: Japan and Germany, despite restrictions on their military, were in the market for planes that could be part of their new defensive strategy. The problem for Lockheed's salesmen was that the plane they had to offer was neither an elegant jet fighter nor a versatile showcase of new military technology, but rather an awkward combination of both.

Since they had difficulty persuading governments to place orders for the F-104 strictly on its merits, Lockheed's overseas executives turned to "unorthodox" sales methods. In countries around the world, they found willing partners, middlemen with access to the highest reaches of government, who were able to sway decisions for a price, and with access to a pool of funds that would not be tracked too closely. In the Netherlands, Lockheed acquired the friendship and the services of Prince Bernhardt, who had married into the Dutch royal family, and who accepted payments through a variety of middlemen. In Japan, the company worked with a secret agent named Yoshio Kadama, a hard-line nationalist and underworld figure who had been imprisoned by the Americans for war crimes, but who emerged in the 1950s and 1960s as a close associate of more than one prime minister. In Indonesia, Lockheed made generous contributions to a "Widows and Orphans Fund" with close ties to higher-ups in AURI, the Indonesian Air Force. In Italy, various political parties were beneficiaries of Lockheed's largesse. In Saudi Arabia, Lockheed did business with Adnan Khashoggi, later to become famous as one of President Richard Nixon's closest supporters and associates.[2] In the end, Lockheed sold more than 2,000 Starfighters overseas; it managed to sell fewer than 300 to the U.S. Air Force.

Not all of these overseas activities were illegal, and many of them were typical of the era and the industry. There was and still is a customary practice in the defense industry of using overseas "agents" to facilitate contracts with governments. In the 1950s and 1960s, bribery was widely accepted as part of "the cost of doing business." At the time, bribery *overseas* was not even illegal under American law; corporations doing business in other countries were presumed to be subject to the laws (or lack of laws) in those places. The American government and the public at large turned a blind eye to undisclosed cash payments and other clandestine deals that helped sell U.S. products. In the case of the Starfighter, the tactics worked: Lockheed eventually sold a modest number of the planes. It never became the huge hit that the company had initially hoped for, but questionable business practices helped prevent, at least, a financial disaster. With the marketing campaign for the Starfighter, Lockheed had taken a series of steps into murky terrain. These measures succeeded for the company because of secrecy, but also because the prevailing norms were in a state of flux.

Then the company went too far. In the 1960s, Lockheed took another large gamble when it made a decision to enter the commercial jumbo jet market. Boeing was in the process of launching what would become one of the greatest commercial jet successes of all time, the 747. Lockheed decided to try to keep pace by developing a plane that was slightly smaller than the 747, and that might therefore be more economical for the U.S. domestic market, while still attractive as an overseas flier. Late to the game, the company had fierce and direct competition from another major player, McDonnell-Douglas, which was developing the DC-10. It was clear to some industry observers early on that the potential market could not support two competitors. But by this time, Lockheed had poured vast sums into the research and development of its entry, the L-1011 TriStar. Since this was a commercial project, Lockheed had invested its own money, not that of the U.S. government. The corporation was going to need to sell a lot of TriStars to get it back. Intense salesmanship produced a modest number of orders from the American airlines. TWA and American agreed to buy a few, but when the biggest U.S. carrier, United, decided to go with the DC-10, Lockheed had to concede defeat in the U.S. market. As with the Starfighter, the company was forced to look abroad.

With Lockheed's finances in disarray, and its global reputation on the line, the company's vice-chairman, Carl Kotchian, took up residence in Tokyo in the fall of 1972 in a desperate attempt to persuade the major Japanese airlines that the L-1011 was their future. Lockheed once again engaged the services of the ultranationalist Yoshio Kadama, and soon money was changing hands, sometimes in the form of corrugated orange cardboard boxes and airline flight bags stuffed with thousands of 10,000-yen notes. The Japanese companies had been leaning toward the DC-10; indeed, before Kotchian arrived, the largest airline, JAL, had already struck a tentative deal with McDonnell-Douglas. But Kotchian's cash and connections helped turn the tide. After seventy days of intensive lobbying, involving not only the companies themselves but also the intervention of officials at the highest level of the Japanese government, Kotchian won a victory of sorts. He left Japan with orders for twenty-one TriStars, and he returned a hero to Lockheed's California headquarters.

Three years later, however, it all unraveled. First Lockheed's auditors started raising questions about large expenditures that could not be accounted for. (Why *was* the company suddenly so extraordinarily generous to the widows and orphans of Indonesia?) For a time, the company's management successfully deflected those questions, but once the stories started to reach the Securities and Exchange Commission and the U.S.

Congress, the spotlight began to shine into the darkest corners of Lockheed's business. In 1975, the Senate Subcommittee on Multinationals, under the chairmanship of Frank Church of Idaho, began hearings on the political connections of major American corporations. The subcommittee's work began as a post-Watergate investigation, focused on how American business leaders had supported Richard Nixon's corrupt Committee to Re-Elect the President (CREEP). But the defense contractors' overseas dealings quickly came to their attention. Tom Jones, the CEO of rival Northrop, casually told the subcommittee that his company had modeled its overseas sales program on Lockheed. Senate investigators took the hint, and by the summer of 1975, Lockheed was the center of the subcommittee's focus and in the headlines of every American newspaper.

The Church Committee brought to light the whole tawdry network of secret deals, political favors, and outright bribery that stretched back into the 1950s. Lockheed was not the only player in the aeronautics industry to engage in these activities, nor was it the only one to receive government scrutiny. But the sheer size of the company, the scope of its international activities, and the harsh spotlight of the subcommittee combined to make Lockheed a watchword for global bribery. The investigations in the United States touched off similar inquiries around the world: There were Lockheed scandals in Italy, the Netherlands, and Japan. In Japan, the investigation eventually revealed the personal involvement of Prime Minister Kakuei Tanaka with Carl Kotchian's 1972 campaign for the TriStar. Tanaka was forced to resign in disgrace, and he was later convicted on bribery charges.

Lockheed became a byword for the shady practices of American multinational corporations, and a major impetus for new legislation that, at long last, put the onus on American companies for their own behavior, even when operating outside of the United States. In the wake of the scandal, Lockheed's top management, including vice-chairman Carl Kotchian and CEO Dan Haughton, were forced to resign. While taking the fall, both men were clearly somewhat baffled by the turn of events. They had been operating under a set of rules that had appeared to them to allow a certain amount of latitude at the boundaries. Kotchian, in particular, steadfastly maintained his conviction that the prurient examination of business practices had done more harm than good, that the shady dealings around the edges of global salesmanship were insignificant in comparison to the good that was done by saving jobs and, perhaps, saving the financial viability of the corporation. Kotchian justified the bribes as the "admission to a ball game," complained that Lockheed had been made a "scapegoat," and compared himself to a beleaguered Richard Nixon.[3]

By their own light, Lockheed's senior executives had operated within the boundaries of ethics as they understood it. Who was hurt by the payments? The competitors, of course, but what was unethical about beating out competition that was playing by the same rules? Lockheed did not have an internal ethics program in the 1960s and 1970s. But if it had had one, it is unlikely that global business dealings would even have been a topic for discussion. Carl Kotchian and Dan Haughton were operating in an environment where senior executives were admired for "pushing the envelope," even if it meant transgressing ethical boundaries. It would have taken a courageous willingness to consider the fundamental aspects of Lockheed's work—the ethics of the tangled relationships between corporations and middlemen and governments—to have challenged these practices from within.

The Brink of Bankruptcy

The overseas bribery scandals by themselves were enough to send Lockheed reeling, but they were not the only major scandal that the company faced during this period of rapid economic and military expansion. On the home front, the cozy interdependence between the defense contractors and the U.S. government gradually came under public scrutiny, finally bursting into the headlines with the disclosure of Operation Illwind in the late 1980s. Lockheed was less prominently at center stage in the overcharging and corruption investigations than it had been in the global bribery scandals. Nevertheless, the company (and many of the "heritage companies" that make up Lockheed Martin today) were embedded in a process of doing business with the Pentagon that was finally exposed as deeply tainted. The American taxpayer was footing the bill for long-term practices that served the interests of big defense contractors and corrupt members of the Pentagon brass. The public relations costs of these scandals, even more than the bribery escapades, paved the way for the development of Lockheed's ethics program.

This part of the story began in the early 1960s, with a well-intentioned program initiated in the Kennedy administration by Secretary of Defense Robert McNamara. The Defense Department recognized that the pace of the Cold War buildup and the increasingly complex nature of national security technology were creating an enormous problem with cost overruns. Under current practice, the Defense Department would select a contractor to develop a particular plane or weapons system, but the final cost of the design, construction, and delivery of the product would be undetermined. With so many variables affecting the cost, contractors naturally preferred to have significant wiggle room to be able to recover the enormous research and development expenses. The problem was that once a contractor was signed on and the government had committed tens of millions of dollars to a project, it was difficult to say no to a company that pleaded for more investment to deliver the product.

Robert McNamara's team proposed and implemented a response to this problem; they called it Total Package Pricing (TPP). Under TPP, the relevant branch of the military would issue a request for proposals, and contractors would be required to submit a bid with a single price for the entire package. The costs would be known in advance, and the contractors would no longer be able to pad their profit margins along the way. The program responded to long-standing American public concerns about excessive profits for wartime and military expenditures.

In 1965, the U.S. Air Force completed the proposal process for a major new project, a transport jet of such size and power that it would dwarf any other military aircraft that had ever been built. The Pentagon wanted a plane that could carry more soldiers farther and faster than any plane in history. Not only were the technical requirements daunting, the project would be completed under the new TPP guidelines. Uneasy about the new rules but unable to resist the lure of a major new project, three defense giants submitted bids. Lockheed, betting that it could complete the project for $1.8 billion, was awarded the contract.

Lockheed succeeded in engineering terms, producing the world's largest airplane, but in economic terms, the development of the C-5 (Galaxy) was a disaster. For a start, the technical challenges of the Air Force's request were daunting and required much more time and effort to solve than Kelly Johnson and his engineers had anticipated. (When completed, a loaded Galaxy weighed in at more than 400 tons, nearly twice the size of the L-1011 jumbo passenger jet.) A series of other factors drove up the cost of the project: constant changes to the design that the Air Force imposed along the way, the rapid inflation of the Vietnam era, and Lockheed's own poor management practices. Over three years of development, the cost of the project nearly tripled, to $5.2 billion. It proved impossible for the U.S. government to hold Lockheed strictly to the terms of the original contract. So despite the original intent of TPP, the Pentagon subsidized most of the cost of the development of the Galaxy, through a series of bargains and concessions that worked around the terms of the original agreement.[4] The payments, however, were not enough to meet Lockheed's true costs, so the company was still bleeding money on the Galaxy. At the same time, the U.S. taxpayer was footing the bill for cost overruns again.

These practices came to the attention of Wisconsin Senator William Proxmire, a legendary watchdog on government expenditures. Proxmire's Joint Economic Committee exposed the Total Package Price fiction, with Lockheed's Galaxy as his leading exhibit. Proxmire painted Lockheed and other defense contractors as pigs continuing to feed at the public trough, even though the amount of food in the trough was supposed to be rationed. In the end, public pressure forced the Defense Department and Lockheed to negotiate a final settlement in which the corporation suffered a financial loss of $250 million. The government had subsidized most of the cost overruns for the Galaxy, but the size of the settlement nevertheless sent Lockheed reeling. The company had simultaneously gone over budget on several other projects besides the Galaxy. By the time all the settlements were reached, Lockheed had suffered a loss of nearly half a billion dollars. These settlements, combined with the financial setbacks associated with the development of the commercial L-1011, pushed Lockheed to the edge of bankruptcy in the first months of 1970. It took a $250-million loan guarantee from the U.S. government to keep the company solvent.

Lockheed saw itself as a victim of policies and circumstances, a scapegoat for an uninformed Congressional and public understanding of the nature of its business. As with the bribery scandals, the company saw itself as operating in a way that was necessary in a competitive marketplace. The special and curious relationship between the corporation and its biggest customer was not viewed as an ethics issue, but simply as an inherent part of the company's particular business. Critics of Lockheed and the defense industry saw it differently; in the latest wave of concern over special favors, there were even calls to nationalize the major arms contractors.[5]

One casualty of the process was the whole concept of Total Package Pricing. The Galaxy was a spectacular example, but many other projects of the era ended up needing subsidies that defeated the whole purpose of the TPP idea. If anything, the failure of TPP reinforced the idea that the Defense Department had to help its biggest suppliers stay in business, and that protecting profit margins required accounting creativity. The stage was set for the next wave of scandals, during the presidency of Ronald Reagan.

Lockheed barely survived the scandals and the financial crisis of the 1970s, but the company emerged from the edge of bankruptcy and prospered during the 1980s, when Reagan's determination to win the Cold War prompted escalating defense budgets. The company's new management, led by CEO Roy Anderson, quickly distanced itself from the excesses of the past and focused on decentralizing Lockheed's structure, to provide both more independence and accountability for managers and engineering teams. Kelly Johnson retired as the head of the Skunk Works; he was succeeded by his protégé Ben Rich, who lacked Johnson's genius but also brought a lighter touch to the human relations part of the job. The scandals had brought more vigorous government involvement and oversight to the company's engineering projects. Johnson's penchant for secrecy had to be modified in the new era, as the circle of people inside and outside the company who had to be "in the know" about Skunk Works projects expanded.

The project that restored glamour and profits to Lockheed was the Stealth fighter jet. The F-117, with its black exterior, streamlined body, and explosive speed, was designed to literally go off the radar screen. It represented a triumph of military technology. This project, along with the steady success of the company's missile and space businesses, swiftly turned around Lockheed's fortunes. By the mid-1980s, the company was confident enough to begin a buying spree, as consolidations and spin-offs began to characterize the defense industry. The biggest prize was the acquisition in 1992 of the division of General Dynamics that produced the durable and popular F-16 fighter jet, adding a huge new manufacturing facility in Fort Worth, Texas, to Lockheed's capacity.

In the midst of these successes, however, a new set of unsavory practices in the defense industry was exposed to public view. First came the
overcharging scandals. The helter-skelter spending of the military buildup had made it easy for contractors to pad their expenses, especially by
assigning grotesquely inflated markups to parts and supplies. In 1985,
when Congressional attention brought the details to light, stories leaked
out about $400 hammers, $600 toilet seats, and a pair of pliers that cost
the American taxpayer $2,000. A coffee brewer on Lockheed's C-5A
transport jet was priced at $7,400, because the Air Force insisted that it
had to be tough enough to withstand a crash. A host of related practices
came to light at the same time: billing for babysitting for executives' children, country-club fees and sumptuous dinners, and even kennel fees
for an executive's dog. Felony prosecutions followed. Half of the Pentagon's top one hundred suppliers were under criminal investigation in
1985; the cases were so egregious that they mobilized Ronald Reagan's Justice Department. Republican Senator Barry Goldwater, usually a staunch
defender of the military establishment, was heard to call Defense Secretary Casper Weinberger "a goddamned fool" for letting the expenditures
get out of hand.[6]

These revelations were damaging enough, but by the end of the decade,
investigators uncovered an even more sinister pattern of corruption. In
1986, a low-level military consultant named John Marlowe, convicted of
molesting a pair of children in a basement in Arlington, Virginia, turned
informant for the Justice Department. The information that Marlowe
provided launched Operation Illwind, which uncovered the most bla-
tant graft in the higher reaches of the U.S. government since the Teapot
Dome scandals of the 1920s. As portrayed in dozens of cases that the
government brought against contractors and individuals in the defense
establishment, both inside and outside of government, the cozy personal
relationships between government and industry carried with them a
web of favors, secret deals, and in some cases outright bribery.

This new wave of scandals did not catch the defense industry un-
prepared. Sensitized by now to the cost of investigations and bad press,
the "bad apple" defense became the favored tactic. One notable case involved a low-level financial analyst named Richard Fowler, who used his
friendship with colleagues at his former employer, the Department of
Defense, to funnel hundreds of documents into the hands of his new

employer, the Boeing Corporation. Fowler undertook these activities for nearly a decade, providing Boeing with inside information handy for bidding on contracts and keeping tabs on the competition. Once his misdeeds were exposed, however, the company closed ranks, insisting that Fowler had operated alone. Boeing's internal investigations ended with mild admonishments for some of Fowler's superiors; in the end, he faced the justice system alone.

In comparison to Boeing and other contractors, Lockheed itself managed to remain out of the limelight during Operation Illwind. Some of the entities, however, that would eventually become part of today's Lockheed Martin did not escape scrutiny. The CEO of Martin Marietta, Tom Pownall, maintained a close relationship with Assistant Secretary of the Navy Melvin Paisley, the most senior government official to be indicted and convicted in the scandal. Pownall, cultivating this friendship at a time when Martin Marietta's defense business was growing rapidly, arranged for financing for improvements to Paisley's Washington home and appeared to benefit from the relationship. Pownall himself never came under indictment, but the shadow of the scandal fell over his company.

By the early 1990s, Operation Illwind had produced ninety convictions of individuals and companies, but it also produced a strange mismatch between the scope of the investigation and the attitude of those under its scrutiny. The operation had exposed a culture of favors and cooperation and looking the other way that extended to the highest reaches of both industry and government. The problem was clearly *systemic,* an extension of the ways that American companies had bent rules together for mutual advantage for more than a century. Yet the defense industry continued to insist on the "bad apple" defense. "I don't know of any city of 90,000 that doesn't have a police force and a jail," said Lockheed's chairman, Roy Anderson.[7] The industry was finally ready to turn its attention to ethics, but its focus would be on individual misdeeds, not on the ethics of corporate culture.

The Emergence of Principle

In May 1977, as Lockheed sought to rebound from the bribery scandals and the Church Committee hearings, the company published a document in its company magazine, *Lockheed Life,* under the title "Lockheed

Principles of Business Conduct." In six brisk paragraphs, the company sought to articulate a set of ideals that would right its ethical ship. "High principles of business conduct must underlie the policies of any corporation," the statement began. "We believe the management of Lockheed has an obligation to articulate the general principles which should guide and motivate the people of Lockheed. We are clearly stating them now as a mark of our determination to conduct the company's business on an ethical basis and as an imperative signal to every man and woman in the corporation that they must share these principles." The statement went on to promise that Lockheed would comply with the laws of the United States and foreign countries, would avoid conflict of interest, would "operate in a manner that is in concert with the objectives of the U.S. Government," and would "strive for integrity in every aspect of our work."

The document explicitly connected right-minded behavior to the success of the company as a whole. "Ethical conduct is the highest form of loyalty to Lockheed," it asserted, making it clear that "it is the responsibility of every man and woman in the corporation to know and accept these principles." The statement promised "continuing attention, guidance and enforcement by management," as the policies in these areas developed and grew.

In some ways, this statement of principles was a bland and timid start to Lockheed's ethics program. General promises to obey the law and to observe the wishes of the American government were easy to articulate, but equally easy to ignore. Although the company's two top executives had resigned in the wake of the bribery investigations, the internal housecleaning that followed their departure was not extensive. Assigning responsibility for knowing and accepting these principles to "every man and woman in the company" could be seen as a way of diffusing responsibility so widely that no one would be truly accountable.

Nevertheless, Lockheed's first, tentative attempt at a code of ethics, like others that major corporations were adopting in the 1970s, represented an important shift in thinking. Americans had always been concerned with the social and ethical behavior of individual "businessmen." The language of business ethics had focused on the actions and intentions of individual corporate leaders—acting in their business capacity, of course, but acting as individuals who had the power and could develop the will to conduct their work in accordance with the highest moral principles. Underlying this emphasis on personal morality was an unspoken assumption. Corporations, especially large corporations, operated in something like a state of nature. Their actions and activities as collective entities would inevitably put self-interest ahead of virtue. If corporations behaved responsibly, it was either because responsible behavior happened to conform to maximizing profits, or because a virtuous corporate leader was willing to put ethics ahead of the bottom line.

The Lockheed code changes that balance. Of course, there is still a role for management in guiding and enforcing ethical behavior, but the document sets a standard of behavior for the corporation as a whole. Could a massive entity of fifty thousand, a hundred thousand, two hundred thousand people embody a lofty set of principles, while earning salaries for its workers and creating wealth for its stockholders? This was the challenge that Lockheed said that it would meet.

As the overcharging and corruption scandals of the 1980s came to public attention, it became clear that the defense industry as a whole had played fast and loose in many different aspects of their business. By the middle of the decade, companies were reeling under the effects of government scrutiny, media attention, and the work of new nonprofits like the Project On Government Oversight (POGO), which began a systematic series of investigations on the excesses of the industry. In early 1986, the President's Blue Ribbon Commission on Defense Management (the Packard Commission) released a sweeping report that charted the fraud and waste within the industry, and that noted that public confidence was at a low.[8] The defense giants had, like Lockheed, responded with statements and codes expressing the best of intentions, but there were strong disincentives for any single company to act too virtuously. There were profits to consider, after all, and it was difficult to give up every competitive advantage for the sake of a higher standard of conduct.

Conscious that they needed a level playing field, the leaders of the American defense industry, including Lockheed, created a pact. Meeting in Washington, D.C., in the spring of 1986, a select group of executives created the Defense Industry Initiative on Business Ethics and Conduct (DII), with the explicit purpose of making it easier for any one company to act ethically since its competitors were promising to do the same. Jack Welch, the hard-driving CEO of General Electric, took the lead, eventually bringing thirty-two of the country's largest contractors to the table to agree to six fundamental principles. The contractors promised to develop and adhere to codes of ethics, to train employees in the codes, to encourage internal reporting of violations, to implement systems to monitor compliance, to share ethics "best practices" with their competitors, and to "be accountable to the public."[9]

As with Lockheed's original code, the principles were modest, but the shift in thinking was extraordinary. The DII was a more comprehensive, more formal version of the industrywide ethics codes that had been developed in much smaller industries in the 1920s and 1930s. Never before had a major sector of the American corporate community agreed to bind its members to a set of ideals to constrain the excesses of their practices. The DII began work as a new type of industry consortium, convening annually to compare notes on progress, and thereby giving corporate leaders new windows into each other's methods. The signatories were eager to trumpet their newfound virtue to their biggest customer and the larger public, but they did so in the face of considerable skepticism. However remarkable the project, the jury was still out on whether the DII represented genuine reform or was simply an elaborate public relations smokescreen.

As a DII signatory, Lockheed began to formalize its ethics program and to insert the language of ethics into its corporate culture. Its first efforts were based on the premise that employees simply needed to be reminded of the "right thing to do." The code of conduct was duly published, revised, disseminated. A compliance department developed regulations and checklists, and charged supervisors and trainers with delivering lectures to employee teams at which certain mandatory points would be covered. The ethics program proceeded on the assumption that repeating the mantra of legal compliance and "integrity" would minimize risk of misbehavior—and, more importantly, would indemnify the company if anyone were caught. The ethics programs made the "bad apple" defense more plausible. After all, if the company informed employees about the difference between appropriate and inappropriate behavior, then any misdeeds would become a matter of individual wrongdoing, rather than corporate malfeasance.

The indemnification strategy became even more important in 1991, with the strengthening of the U.S. Sentencing Guidelines. The guidelines specified penalties not only for individual criminal behavior, but also for white-collar crimes and various forms of corporate misbehavior. Not only were companies liable for damages for shady business practices, but those that lacked effective business ethics programs would be punished more severely. The guidelines also listed a series of positive requirements that would mitigate corporate penalties, if certain desirable practices were in place.

Lockheed was developing its ethics program at a difficult moment for the company. The end of the Cold War meant a slowdown in defense department contracting, and while the company still had a large backlog of Reagan-era projects to complete, future sources of profits were in doubt. The 1991 Gulf War provided a brief moment of glory, as the high-tech aircraft and weapons systems made by Lockheed and other defense contractors were credited with the ease of the American-led victory over Iraq. Instability reigned in the defense industry, as a dizzying series of mergers and acquisitions changed the face of dozens of companies and the loyalties of hundreds of thousands of workers around the country. Lockheed was a major player in the shakeout, making several key purchases that strengthened its place in the air, space, and missile fields. It was also a target for others; the company narrowly avoided a takeover by Texas businessman Harold C. Simmons in the early 1990s. Faced with these uncertainties, Lockheed ultimately decided that if big was good, much bigger was much better. In 1995, in a top-secret but rapid series of negotiations, the company agreed to a massive "merger of equals" with Martin Marietta.

Like Lockheed, Martin Marietta was the corporate extension of the dreams of an aviation pioneer of the early years of the twentieth century. Glenn Martin had launched his first airplane in Santa Ana, California, in 1909, but after merging with the Wright Company, he eventually moved his base of operations to Ohio. Martin became known for its effective long-range bombers; the company assembled the *Enola Gay,* a Boeing-designed B-29 aircraft, which flew the fateful mission over Hiroshima in 1945. In the postwar years, however, Martin more or less abandoned the crowded aviation field to focus more intensively on weapons systems and space programs. It built missiles for the Pershing and Titan programs, it created the space launch vehicles for Project Gemini and other early manned space flights, and it was a key player in the development of the space shuttle, after its merger with the American-Marietta Company.

Lockheed's merger with Martin Marietta was widely hailed, both inside the companies and by investors, as a rare instance of corporate synergy. The two giants were competitors, but with sufficiently different areas of specialty that overlap would be minimal. The two chief executives, Daniel Tellep of Lockheed and Norman Augustine of Martin Marietta, appeared to get along well, and worked out a succession in which Tellep would become the first CEO of the new company and would gracefully retire after two years to make way for Augustine to take the top spot. Martin Marietta's central office in Bethesda, Maryland, was the natural choice for the new Lockheed Martin headquarters, given the proximity to its largest customer. With nearly 200,000 employees the new Lockheed Martin became the country's largest defense contractor.

The company almost immediately faced another ethics scandal. Apparently the lessons of the 1970s and the inception of an ethics program had not entirely reformed Lockheed's overseas sales techniques. In the late 1980s, Lockheed's representatives, eager to sell a number of its C-130H aircraft to Egypt, made a series of payments to a member of the Egyptian parliament, in exchange for her services in helping to secure the contract. When such practices had come to light in the 1970s, Lockheed had been able to argue, disingenuously but truthfully, that overseas bribery was not illegal under *American* law. But after the 1970s Lockheed scandal, Congress had passed the Foreign Corrupt Practices Act (FCPA) to close that loophole. In 1995, immediately following the Lockheed Martin merger, the company pled guilty to conspiring to bribe the Egyptian official and to falsifying its books to try to cover up the action.[10] The new company was not only hit with a $24 million fine; it was also placed under a three-year administrative agreement that reduced the company's ability to do business with the Pentagon and created a series of standards for the company's ethics program.

Recruiting Dilbert

Norman Augustine became CEO of Lockheed Martin on schedule in 1996. An engineer by background, he began his career at Douglas Aircraft, moved to the Pentagon under Secretary of Defense Robert McNamara, and was in and out of government for several years until settling in at Martin Marietta in 1974. Known for his gregarious personality and homespun wisdom, Augustine rose through the ranks to become Martin Marietta's CEO in 1987, and presided over the merger to form the new Lockheed Martin. Reflective but lighthearted, he had published a book called *Augustine's Laws* in 1983, which was, as he explained later, "dedicated to the proposition that if one had a better understanding of history, one could generate a happy ending—sort of like running a movie backward." His "laws" included such propositions as: "The best way to make a silk purse from a sow's ear is to start with a silk sow. The same is true of money." And: "By the time people asking the questions are ready for the answers, the people doing the work have lost track of the questions."[11]

Ethics rated high on Norm Augustine's agenda. It had to, since Lockheed Martin was operating under the administrative agreement after the Egyptian bribery scandal. But Augustine also had a special passion for the idea of personal integrity. He liked to quote a definition that he attributed to U.S. Supreme Court Justice Potter Stewart: "Ethics is knowing the difference between what you have a right to do and what is the right thing to do."[12] Augustine had a weakness for the illustrative anecdote, many of them drawn from the world of professional sports. Was it right for Ted Williams to refuse a pay raise after he had a below-par season as a hitter? Is it unethical for 50,000 fans at a football game to make noise in order to disrupt the rhythm of the visiting team's quarterback? Does a professional golfer have an obligation to warn his opponent that the latter is about to commit a rule violation? He also enjoyed illustrations from his personal experience at Lockheed Martin, such as the time when he had to reimburse the corporation for an expensive watch that his wife wished to receive as a gift from a supplier. "For most of us, when it comes to ethics," Augustine wrote, "there is a personal Rubicon that, sooner or later, we have to cross. Our personal Rubicon may not be a matter of life or death, but nonetheless we have to recognize that ethical comportment comes before business, before winning, and sometimes even before loyalty."[13]

Augustine recognized that there was a problem with Lockheed Martin's ethics program: It was boring. It was intended to fulfill the requirements of the federal government, but reaching every employee in a corporation of nearly 200,000 represented a special challenge. It was obvious that lectures and checklists were ineffective. More importantly, a dull ethics program was counterproductive, since it stimulated resentment, cynicism, and outright hostility toward the whole idea of ethics. He told the lawyer in charge of Lockheed Martin's ethics program, Carol Marshall, that she had to come up with something better.

Marshall was not quite sure how to change things, but an idea struck her as she was traveling from site to site around the corporation. Everyplace she went, her eye kept catching—on bulletin boards, on office doors, on the walls of tiny cubicles—strips of paper from the Sunday comics. A company drone named Dilbert, and his canine sidekick Dogbert, had struck a chord. It was clear that these comic-strip characters had won the hearts of Lockheed Martin employees more effectively than the ethics program. Perhaps there was a way for ethics to piggyback on Dilbert's success.

Steve Cohen was a specialist in employee training and communication in Boston who was looking for a more powerful way to get messages across to workers in the corporate environment. He, too, had noticed that this new comic strip called *Dilbert* was popping up on walls in the offices of his corporate clients. Besides, he liked the comic strip's irreverent humor; surely something could be made of it. In 1993, Cohen and his partner David Gebler pooled their capital, took out some extra loans, and paid $50,000 for the rights to *Dilbert*. It was a lot of money and a risky venture; the men decided not to tell their wives about the deal. Once the rights were in hand, Cohen and Gebler struggled for three years to figure out just how to use the concept most productively.

Then one day in 1996, Steve Cohen got a call from Paul Haney, Carol Marshall's second-in-command at the Lockheed Martin ethics office. Haney was inquiring about the *Dilbert* rights. Would Cohen Gebler consider working with Lockheed Martin on an ethics program with *Dilbert* at its center? Steve Cohen had had little exposure to corporate ethics, and even less to the defense industry, but it did not take long to say yes to a $20-billion corporation.

Working with the Lockheed Martin ethics office, Cohen Gebler took the first steps, creating an internal marketing campaign to illustrate the concept. They developed a poster featuring Dogbert living it up on company time, and they tried it out on a group of Lockheed Martin executives. The first reaction was not encouraging. "We're under the threat of indictment by the federal government," one manager said, "and the best you can come up with is a comic strip?" Not only was *Dilbert* a comic strip, but its humor aimed straight at the foibles and hypocrisies of corporate culture. Much of the comic strip's punch comes in the form of shots at Dilbert's boss, who cheerfully and conspicuously puts his own interests and occasionally those of the company ahead of Dilbert and other low-level employees. Lockheed's corporate culture was, perhaps, a little more freewheeling than some, but it was going to take a more concerted effort to convince the company that ethics could be sold with so light and cynical a touch. Fortunately for Cohen Gebler, Norm Augustine loved the idea. Overriding the objections of some of his senior team, Augustine gave the order for the development of a full-fledged ethics awareness program with Dilbert at its center. It was clear to Augustine, as well as to Cohen, that the edge of *Dilbert* was an ideal vehicle with which to meet the cynicism that they could expect from employees about a corporate ethics program. It played on the natural mix of admiration and ambivalence that Americans, especially those in an independent engineering culture, brought to the structure and rituals of corporate life.

With this initial backing of senior management, Cohen Gebler went to work designing a format for a *Dilbert*-based ethics awareness program. Steve Cohen borrowed the idea of an ethics board game from a program that had been in place at Martin Marietta, a concept called "Gray Matters." The game part was a good idea, he thought; the problem was that the presentation had itself been gray and lifeless. Cohen spent some time rambling through the games sections of toy stores, seeking inspiration. The result was, eventually, "The Ethics Challenge," which became the mandatory ethics awareness program for every employee at Lockheed Martin in 1997.

"The Ethics Challenge" came in a bright yellow box, of the same size and shape as "Monopoly" or "Clue." Indeed, the concept for the game board was pretty obviously lifted from "Clue" itself. Fifteen by fifteen squares, its most prominent feature was a series of "rooms," but instead of the "parlor" and the "dining room," players moved in and out of the "conference room," the "boss's office," and the "cafeteria." At the start of the game, each room held three "ethics challenge tokens."

Every Lockheed Martin manager was responsible for serving as the "leader" of an hour-long "Ethics Challenge" game. The company organized this in a "cascade-down" fashion, beginning with CEO Norm

Augustine and his senior staff. Those staff members would, in turn, lead subsequent sessions with the managers who reported to them, so each manager (except the CEO!) would have the experience of playing the game as an ordinary team member, before serving as the training leader.

The training leader assembled a group of at least six and no more than forty-two employees to play the game. Depending on the number of players, the leader divided the group up into teams of at least three players, so each game was played with up to six teams. Each team chose one of the *Dilbert* characters (Dilbert, Wally, Ratbert, Catbert, The Boss, and Alice) as its playing piece, and found the appropriate starting place on the game board. The leader then played the introductory video, which featured CEO Norm Augustine and instructions on the rules from Dogbert. Then they were off and running.

To begin a "move," each team selected one of fifty "case file cards." Each card contained an ethics issue or dilemma, drawn from the actual experience of Lockheed Martin ethics officers and employees. One team member read the case aloud, and presented the group with four possible responses. Teams then discussed the case and decided on the best "ethical" response to the case.

"The brother-in-law of your boss works for him," Case 22 began[14] "and lately [he] seems to be getting the easy assignments. You've also noticed that he is driving a new car and bragging about a recent pay raise. Should you be concerned or just mind your own business?" The guide contained four potential answers: (A) to talk with your Human Resources representative; (B) to go to the next level of management above the boss; (C) "Ignore it—it's none of your business"; or (D) to confront the brother-in-law and ask him about his raise. (At the bottom of the page, Dogbert offers his thought: "Ask your boss if you can date his other sister.") Team members were instructed to bat this case around for five minutes and then propose their best answer. Once all teams reported their answers, each would be awarded a certain number of points. For Case 22, a team would receive five points for going to Human Resources, three points for going over the boss's head, and zero points for the less proactive responses of ignoring the situation or person-to-person confrontation.

Team members were instructed to base their responses on the six "company values" and an "ethical decision-making model" found in the front of their team guide. The six values—honesty, integrity, respect, trust, responsibility, and citizenship—were defined in the booklet and were promoted as pillars of the way that Lockheed Martin does business. The "Ethical Decision Making Model" asked employees to: "1) evaluate information; 2) consider how your decision might affect stakeholders; 3) consider what ethical values are relevant to the situation; and 4) determine the best course of action that takes into account relevant values and stakeholders' interests."

A team could "win" the game by traveling around the board quickly enough to collect tokens from each of the various "rooms." Over the course of an hour, a team might have a chance to discuss a series of situations. What do you do when your manager "'chews you out' at length and in very loud, abusive, demeaning terms?" How do you handle a situation where your supervisor directs you not to inspect flight hardware but to stamp it off as having been replaced? (Dogbert says: "Advise your friends not to fly.") What should you do when your boss gently touches you on the thigh when you're sharing a cab on way back from the airport? Do you need to report it when your daughter starts a business of making promotional t-shirts and solicits Lockheed Martin as a client?

Victory was supposed to be secondary to interactive discussion. "The Ethics Challenge" turned ethics awareness from a set of rules into a process, where certain guidelines prevailed and where some answers were clearly wrong, but where there were enough gray areas for people to argue about their choices. Through its format and its content, the game acknowledged that the ethics of business conduct involved difficult decisions, in a world where employees were under pressure to perform at a high level and at maximum speed.

Cohen Gebler used the *Dilbert* characters to leaven the process with irreverent humor, anticipating employee cynicism about ethics and giving it a natural, self-deprecating outlet. Dilbert and Dogbert rudely interrupt Norm Augustine during his introduction on the video, inviting an open season for poking fun at management's preachiness. Dogbert's sarcastic responses further respond to and contain employee cynicism, sometimes by verging on the politically incorrect. In response to the case of a handicapped employee who has been harassed by coworkers who disable her wheelchair and obstruct the ramps, Dogbert advises: "Kneecap the harassers. This will teach them empathy."

On the one hand, the concept of "The Ethics Challenge" was exceedingly modest. After all, it occupied just one hour per year for each employee. Even the company's own note to training leaders acknowledged that employees were sure to notice that an hour per year of ethics paled in comparison to quarterly, monthly, and even daily measurement of performance and financial objectives. Yet on the other hand, the format was hugely ambitious, reaching thousands of employees, and also *engaging* them. "Six months after the first Ethics Challenge," Steve Cohen recalled, "I was walking down the hallway in a Lockheed facility when one of the employees heard that I was the guy who had put together the game. He came over to me and started haranguing me about how I was wrong about the best answer for Case #6. That was when I knew that we had done something right."

The particular genius of the "Ethics Challenge" was that it opened up widespread genuine discussion, while at the same time it contained dissent, and confined the discussion of ethics to questions of personal choice and individual responsibility. Ethics, in other words, came down to a series of key choices that individuals would have to make, some times with the assistance of particular corporate offices. The game scored some clear successes in creating awareness of the company's rhetoric on values, and in creating a sense that attention to ethics was part of the job of every Lockheed Martin employee. But was this enough to counterbalance the immense forces that had led Lockheed and many other defense giants into one scandal after another over the previous four decades?

The Ethics Challenge was only one piece of Lockheed Martin's efforts to upgrade its ethics program. With Dilbert and Dogbert attracting attention, the company tried to turn a liability—its well-publicized history of scandal—into an asset, through trumpeting its commitment to its reinvigorated ethics program. When Vance Coffman followed Norm Augustine as CEO in 1998, he made it clear that he intended to continue his predecessor's efforts in this area. By the turn of the century, the company's ethics office had evolved from a small, centralized staff concerned principally with issues of compliance with federal regulations, into a corporation-wide network of codes, principles, programs, and people. The company's extensive ethics system built directly on the mode of the "Ethics Challenge": It created a company-wide ethics aura, while at the same time keeping the ethics impulse safely enough within bounds that it could pose no threat to the corporation's pursuit of "mission success."

chapter three

Peeling Back the Onion

CLOSE TO A HUNDRED men and women crowd the Palm Room at the Grand Hyatt Hotel in Orlando, Florida, for the start of the 2003 annual Ethics Officer Conference for the Lockheed Martin Corporation. Clean-cut, casual, welcoming to a new face, ranging in age from their mid-thirties to their early sixties, they are at their ease. The Orlando Hyatt is a big step up from the venue of last year's conference—a colorless facility within easy reach of corporate headquarters in Bethesda—so the mood is upbeat, even if the schedule does not promise much in the way of outings to theme parks. Dress is "business casual." Most of the ethics officers are Caucasian, but there are a respectable number of non-White faces, mostly African Americans, as well.

Some in the crowd are reconnecting with old friends and colleagues, and others are new to the Lockheed ethics world, so the conference begins with an icebreaker: Say something about yourself that no one else knows. After an undertone of ritual complaint about the exercise, they go with the program and settle around their tables to talk, and after fifteen minutes or so report out to the group. Gail at Table 4 once worked on venereal disease issues for the county health services. Rick at Table 6, who works at the Nevada nuclear test site, has 675 birds on his life list; friends know him as the "bird nerd." Rose at Table 8 is revealed to have a "criminal past": She hooked school in third grade. Someone at Table 3 admits that he used to cheat at Scrabble. Mock gasps follow each confession. At Table 3, one officer shows the Scrabble cheater that his actions were in violation of page 2 of the Lockheed Martin Code of Ethics and Business Conduct: "to be honest and forthright with one another."

As the icebreaker winds down, Nancy Higgins takes the podium. The chuckling tones down. In 2003, Ms. Higgins is the vice-president for ethics and business conduct, Lockheed Martin's top ethics officer, and the executive in charge of their whole operation. A woman in her forties, platinum blonde, she sports a broad, toothy smile that seems frozen on her face, even while she is speaking. She calls herself a "recovering lawyer," having moved over from the general counsel's office into the ethics operation at Boeing, before assuming Lockheed Martin's top ethics job in 2001. She speaks slowly, clearly, a bit pedantically, as she moves briskly through a "state of the ethics operation" talk, fortified by Power Point slides sporting Lockheed's flying star logo.

Higgins's speech is a pep talk, reinforcing to her team the value of their work to the corporation. Ethics is a frustrating business, she readily concedes, since people tend really to notice us when things go wrong. But she is happy to cite chapter and verse of the division's accomplishments. The ethics awareness program that really took off with *Dilbert* in 1997 has gone through several reconceptions since then. Calls to ethics officers are up—a sign of confidence in the organization—and more calls than ever are being resolved on the local level, without any formal action being necessary. Lockheed Martin employees as a whole have given feedback that they think that the ethics program is worthwhile, and senior management continues to trumpet ethics as the corporation's "number one value."

There are challenges, to be sure. Surveys show that too many Lockheed Martin employees still believe that they live under a threat of retaliation if they come forward about ethics violations. It turns out that new employees—those who have been at the corporation for six months or less—are particularly vulnerable to ethics violations, since they have not yet fully embraced the company culture. Managers are sometimes turning a deaf ear to ethics concerns raised by those who report to them; sometimes, apparently, managers do not even recognize an ethics issue right under their noses. These challenges, however, are simply next year's work, as the ethics division strives for continuous improvement.

Most importantly, ethics is not simply an activity to fulfill a legal requirement; it is a "value-added" component of the company's mission. Part of Higgins's rhetoric is defensive: Like other divisions that are not "profit centers," the ethics and business conduct division constantly has to prove its worth in a bottom-line business. So Higgins cites the confidence that "the Customer" (the U.S. government) has acquired in Lockheed Martin's integrity as a key to winning new contracts, and she makes broad claims about the savings realized thanks to the prevention of waste and fraud. Yet the real value added is larger and grander than new contracts and dollars saved. It is an almost metaphysical infusion of goodness into the company's products: the fighter jets, the space shuttle, the missile and control systems, the hardware and the software. Ethics, in Higgins's vision, expands and extends Lockheed Martin's "mission success."

The Designers

Lockheed Martin's division of ethics and business conduct is based at the company's headquarters in Bethesda, Maryland. The building, a gray concrete box surrounded by manicured lawns and artificial ponds, gives the feeling of a secluded enclave, rather than a complex in the heart of a suburban office park. The five-story structure itself, with its wide hallways and large windows, has the feeling of an oversized child's play set, with big pieces made for stubby fingers: easy to snap together, easy to take apart, and easy to fashion a new arrangement of the parts that looks, in the end, just like the last construction.

Maryanne Lavan, Lockheed Martin's vice-president of ethics and business conduct as of 2004, oversees an operation that is both highly centralized and conspicuously far-flung. Four senior members of the division work along the second floor hallway in corporate headquarters. Here, the company's ethics policies and programs are designed and refined, and then disseminated to the hundreds of sites that Lockheed Martin maintains in the United States and around the world. Here is where the company-wide ethics "help line" rings. Here is where consultant Steve Cohen comes each winter to help the corporate ethics staff develop next year's "awareness" program.

Beyond Bethesda lie the five "business areas" that make up the corporation. Each business area has an ethics "director," who jointly reports to the vice president of ethics and business conduct back at corporate headquarters, but who also reports to the business area president. These directors are the primary executives for ethics within their business areas, and they also serve as a kind of cabinet for the vice-president, taking turns with leadership on companywide initiatives. In turn, each business area director supervises a group of ethics officers, who are strategically spread out across the corporation's facilities. There are approximately sixty-five ethics officers across the Lockheed Martin world. Many are full-time; some work in related areas like audit or human resources, and the ethics job is only part of their portfolio. An ethics officer's area of responsibility may be a single large facility, or it could include dozens of small facilities scattered over thousands of miles. Seeing so many ethics officers together at the Orlando Grant Hyatt makes them look like a small army of virtue, but the math works out to just one officer for every 2,000 Lockheed Martin employees.[1]

Maryanne Lavan and other Lockheed Martin officials will not specify the precise budget for the Lockheed Martin ethics and business conduct program. She will say only that the figure is in "the millions," especially if the calculation includes the labor costs of the time spent by thousands of corporation personnel who participate in regular ethics trainings. At the Boeing Corporation, whose workforce is approximately 20% larger than Lockheed Martin's, the annual budget for the ethics and business conduct division was $7.6 million in 2003, although Boeing significantly overspent the budget that year in the wake of large-scale ethics scandals.[2]

In practice, then, Lockheed Martin ethics officers work in isolation from one another, immersed in the particular problems of local facilities, working at the behest of company executives who share supervision of the officers with the business area directors. They are men and women who have come through the Lockheed Martin ranks, who have found their way into ethics work through the door of human resources or auditing or perhaps engineering. It is a thin, scattered band, so the burden of spreading consistency through the operation falls on the team at corporate headquarters in Bethesda.

The man primarily responsible for creating the day-to-day aspects of Lockheed Martin's ethics awareness program is Brian Sears, an ethics veteran whose zeal and experience typify the operation. Well over six feet tall, with broad shoulders and a vigorous gait, Sears towers over most of his colleagues at the ethics officers' conference and along the corridors in Bethesda. His low-key manner does little to disguise an active, self-deprecating sense of humor. When I visited him in November 2003, he was busy mock complaining to anyone who would listen that Michael Sears, the chief financial officer at Boeing who had just been fired for ethics improprieties, was "besmirching my good name." His office on the second floor of corporate headquarters shows the habits of a brainstormer: piles of papers on the desk, boxes of ethics surveys cluttering the floors, and a whiteboard crisscrossed with diagrams and slogans for the next ethics awareness project.

Growing up in modest circumstances in the San Joaquin Valley of California, young Brian Sears harbored an ambition to become a writer. He won his first writing contest in sixth grade, edited his high school newspaper, and wrote for the UCLA *Daily Bruin* in college. But he recognized early on that making a living by the pen was uncertain at best. Besides, he was charmed by the romance of flight, and he dreamed of becoming a pilot. He won a Reserve Officers Training Corps (ROTC) scholarship at UCLA in the late 1970s, and he began studying to become a flight navigator. Even in college, however, his big frame was still growing, and after two years of training, his commanding officer delivered the bad news: Sears had grown too much. At six feet six inches, he was too tall for the fighter jets. "If you're over the height limit," he recalls, "when you have to eject from the plane, you lose your kneecaps." He received an honorable medical discharge ("I still have the certificate to prove it"), and he had at least the satisfaction of receiving two free years of education.

Sears had been studying economics at UCLA, but once a career in flight was no longer an option, he wanted something more practical, so he switched to California Polytechnic University in San Luis Obispo to study accounting. It was there that he discovered a new passion: the improbable romance of auditing. The transfer of allegiance from piloting to running numbers might seem unlikely, but the underlying motivation was the same: the allure of travel. His Cal Poly auditing professor spent a great deal of class time describing his overseas consulting assignments for multinational corporations. Brian Sears wanted to see the world; if he could not fly the planes himself, at least he would ride them at someone else's expense.

He took his first job with the Burroughs Corporation in 1980, and he spent more than 90 percent of his time on the road over the next two and a half years. He found that that he loved the travel, but also the numbers. There was something satisfying about their clarity and their precision, and he loved straightening out the inconsistencies in the corporation's books. His professor had called auditing "the art of aggressive diplomacy," which appealed to him.

By 1982, Sears had taken a job in the corporate audit department at Lockheed Corporation. It meant less day-to-day travel, but also being at the service of a national operation. Over the next fifteen years, he moved from Burbank, California, to Austin, Texas, back to Burbank, to Titusville, Florida, and then to the old General Dynamics plant in Fort Worth, Texas. Along the way, he was promoted to audit supervisor, and eventually to a regional manager position in corporate audit.

In 1998, Carol Marshall, then in charge of the Lockheed Martin ethics program, asked him to give a talk to her senior staff on how the internal audit department would measure the efficacy of a compliance training program. Sears had no idea how to grapple with this. He was used to the reliable world of spreadsheets; there were no guideposts about how to evaluate the success and integrity of programs intended to coach employees in complying with federal laws and regulations. "But I gave it my best shot," Sears recalls. "I told a few jokes and improvised." Several months later, he was offered the chance to move from auditing into the ethics operation as a "sector director" for Lockheed's energy business.

Was it strange to make the shift from audit to ethics? Sears insists that the transition was simple and smooth. Auditors, he says, are concerned with doing the right thing. The mind set of checking the facts carefully and weighing all the relevant factors, the familiarity with the basic procedures of investigation, the management experience he had gained as he had climbed through the ranks—these were habits and experiences that served him well as he moved into the ethics operation. The main difference was a wider scope of problems to look into, and, more importantly, the opportunity to be part of a more service-oriented sector of the corporation. "It was just putting on a different hat," he says. "One where I could help people."

In October 1998, Sears and his family moved once again, this time to rural Maryland, giving him a long but manageable commute to the Bethesda headquarters. Starting in the energy area, he moved over to aeronautics, and then became the chief ethics officer for the corporate division itself, meaning that ethics issues involving the corporation's headquarters staff fell within his domain. In 2004, his title changed to

director of ethics awareness for Lockheed Martin as a whole, although
he also retains his corporate ethics officer duties. He is now the principal developer of several of the corporation's new initiatives in the ethics
area, including oversight of the annual training program.

Like everyone else in the Lockheed Martin operation, Sears has no formal training in ethics, nor does such training strike him as necessary or
productive. "It's mostly about developing a set of core values, and living by
them," he says, and that seems to suffice for him as a definition of ethics.
He spends a lot of time trying to communicate the message that ethics is
not just about distinguishing between right and wrong, but that it's about
"the gray area of conflicting values, the difference between right and
right." He concedes that "we might not have a nice, clean answer to every
question." Sears is not inclined to sweat over ethics in the abstract. He believes that a definition of ethics can and should percolate from the bottom
up. "Everyone has their own perspective on ethics," he says. "Who am I to
tell an employee what is or what isn't an ethics issue?" He is eager to move
from beliefs and convictions to the much more practical discussion of the
range of the company's programs and the "robust" quality of its offerings.

Sears is particularly preoccupied—he says "obsessed"—with the connection between the ethics operation and the corporation's competitive
advantage. Mulling over the corporation's 2004 ethics awareness program, he came up with the idea of an "ethics meter" that would graphi-
cally demonstrate the connections between virtuous behavior and tangible benefits for the individual employee and the corporation. A rough
diagram on the whiteboard in his office displays a timeline of a fictional
employee's career, showing how at critical turning points good ethics
leads the way to promotions for the employee, more business for his division, and a better crop of potential employees who are, in theory, attracted to Lockheed Martin's reputation for integrity. Sears is also
painfully aware of the fragility of an ethics operation, of how quickly
confidence in its effectiveness can erode. "Any one person or small group
of people can shut us down," he muses. "All of our efforts can't preclude
the rogue elephant out there."

Brian Sears's sensibility both reflects and affects the tone of the division: practical, easygoing, nondogmatic, inclined to think of ethics as
much as a service operation as a watchdog. Ethics, in the world of Brian

Sears, should be clear, simple, and measurable. Yes, employees face tough dilemmas, but the corporation's support structure should be more than adequate to work through them. Even more, ethics should provide a sense of meaning and mission for a Lockheed Martin employee's work. It should be, at best, a driver, a purpose. Sears is unapologetic about this sense of mission. "We want employees to think: At the end of the career, what is your ethics legacy?" While he is nowhere near retirement, Sears takes pride that his work in the ethics department has already "built value" into the Lockheed Martin empire.

The Code

Brian Sears, and every other ethics officer at Lockheed Martin, bases his work on a foundational document: *Setting the Standard: The Lockheed Martin Code of Ethics and Business Conduct.* First printed immediately following the merger in 1995, the code, updated every year or two, exists in the form of a spiral-bound, pocket-sized booklet, intended for handy reference. Its fifty-four pages are laid out more like a little marketing brochure than a dry legal document, complete with full-page color photos of Lockheed Martin people and products. On page 53 is the "receipt and acknowledgment" form; with each new edition, every Lockheed Martin employee agrees that "I understand that each Lockheed Martin employee, member of the Board of Directors, agent, consultant or contract worker is responsible for knowing and adhering to the principles and standards of the Code." In addition to English, the booklet is available in Arabic, Chinese (Mandarin and Traditional), French, German, Greek, Hebrew, Hungarian, Japanese, Korean, Portuguese, Russian, Spanish, and Turkish.

Public and widely disseminated codes of ethics like *Setting the Standard* are a commonplace now in corporate America. For one thing, they are a basic requirement under the federal sentencing guidelines, Sarbanes–Oxley, and other legislation aimed at promoting corporate accountability and responsibility. A written code is a starting point, the bare minimum for establishing standards. Companies—even small ones—that neglect to write and distribute a code do so at their peril, since the existence of the written document is the first (although minimal) line of defense against lawsuits or criminal investigations that hold top management accountable for illegal or unethical activity.

With increasing scrutiny, the mere existence of a code of business conduct is no longer sufficient; the content and, indeed, the style of such codes have come to matter a great deal. Companies may be tempted to develop a long, dry, excruciatingly detailed list of rules, regulations, and "don'ts," thinking that exhaustiveness can immunize them against every conceivable form of wrongdoing. But observers now pay attention not only to the content of the code, but also to its perceived accessibility. If a document is not readily available and easily read by the average worker, outsiders can charge that it is not an effective means of communicating the ethical bottom line. At the other end of the spectrum, a company that simply lists a few basic values is vulnerable to the charge that its code is no more than vague and empty rhetoric.

Setting the Standard aims to fall between these two poles. Its most striking and insistent feature is that it places responsibility for ethical behavior and for the ethical "performance" of the corporation on each and every individual employee at Lockheed Martin. It begins with a letter from the Chief Executive Officer and the Chief Operating Officer of the corporation, addressed "Dear Colleague," to suggest from the very first line a kind of parity between leadership, management, and line employees. What matters is "the personal integrity of each of our employees and their commitment to the highest standards of personal and professional conduct." The development of an "ethical culture" at Lockheed Martin is based on individual integrity, although in a context "that values teamwork, sets team goals, assumes collective responsibility for actions, embraces diversity, and shares leadership." The letter is intended both to send a message of top-down leadership on the development of this "ethical culture," and to suggest that such a culture is in some sense democratic, built from the bottom of the company up.

The letter spells out the six "principles" through which Lockheed Martin's expects to "set the standard" for ethical behavior:

Honesty: to be truthful in all our endeavors; to be honest and forthright with one another and with our customers, communities, suppliers, and shareholders.

Integrity: to say what we mean, to deliver what we promise, to fulfill our commitments, and to stand for what is right.

Respect: to treat one another with dignity and fairness, appreciating the diversity of our work force and the uniqueness of each employee.

Trust: to build confidence through teamwork and open, candid communication.

Responsibility: to take responsibility for our actions, and to speak up—without fear of retribution—and report concerns in the workplace, including violations of laws, regulations, and company policies, and seek clarification and guidance whenever there is doubt.

Citizenship: to obey all the laws of the United States and other countries in which we do business, and to do our part to make the communities in which we live and work better.

The set of principles is carefully chosen to develop a certain style on which ethics is built, a style that places its signal emphasis on a concept of open communication. Ethics, in the Lockheed Martin conception, develops through the free flow of information—"honesty and forthrightness," "saying what we mean," "candid communication," and a willingness to " speak up" are the networks through which ethics is supposed to flow. The underlying assumption is that the temptation to bend the rules flourishes in isolation, in dark corners and in secrecy, and that frequent and unguarded communication is the best protection against misdeeds. The theory may be sound, but it also poses a particular challenge and strikes an odd chord in a corporate environment where national security concerns and the possibility of corporate espionage make secrecy a paramount necessity.

The bulk of the code, following the opening letter and articulation of the principles, outlines the key topics of concern in maintaining ethics in the Lockheed Martin workplace. The obligation to "PROMOTE A POSITIVE WORK ENVIRONMENT" covers "cultural diversity" and the insistence that "we will not tolerate harassment or discrimination of any kind." (Since 2001, the list of types of discrimination that Lockheed Martin will not tolerate has included sexual orientation and "family structure," in addition to the more established categories. This change, in a conservative company environment, was instituted in response to shareholder pressure at the company's 2000 annual meeting.) "KEEP AC-CURATE AND COMPLETE RECORDS," "MAKE ACCURATE PUBLIC DISCLO-SURES," and "RECORD COSTS PROPERLY" make clear that "no one should rationalize or even consider misrepresenting facts or falsifying records." "AVOID ILLEGAL AND QUESTIONABLE GIFTS OR FAVORS" provides precise detail about federal law and corporate custom on business courtesies. With federal employees, Lockheed Martin representatives can give coffee mugs or calendars, coffee and donuts, or a meal for less than $20; cour-tesies to nongovernment employees simply must be "consistent with marketplace practices, infrequent in nature, and may not be lavish or ex-travagant," and no employee may give or receive a gift worth more than $100. "KNOW THE LAW WHEN INVOLVED IN INTERNATIONAL BUSINESS" focuses less on ethical issues, but calls employees' attention to the U.S. laws that have been enacted in the years since Lockheed was enmeshed in the overseas bribery scandals. Other sections of the code address po-litical contributions ("FOLLOW THE LAW AND USE COMMON SENSE"), conflicts of interest ("STEER CLEAR"), employment of former govern-ment officials ("KNOW THE RULES"), company assets like computers and equipment ("USE WISELY"), and speculative and insider trading ("DO NOT ENGAGE").

At the back of the booklet are a list of "WARNING SIGNS" and a QUICK QUIZ. A Lockheed Martin employee learns there that "YOU'RE ON THIN ETHICAL ICE WHEN YOU HEAR . . ." such phrases as "Well, maybe just this once," or, "It doesn't matter how it gets done as long as it gets done," or, perhaps a bit more obviously, "We didn't have this conversation." Taking the "quiz," employees are instructed, "WHEN IN DOUBT, ASK YOUR-SELF . . ." questions like "How will it look in the newspaper?" and "Will I sleep soundly tonight?" But in case the message has seemed too soft, a section on ACCOUNTABILITY warns that "Violations of the Code are cause for corrective action, which may result in disciplinary action up to and including dismissal." The booklet urges employees to ask and keep asking questions, and provides a list of company resources, including not only the ethics office and the general counsel but also a direct and ostensibly anonymous line of communication to the audit and ethics committee of Lockheed Martin's board of directors.[3]

Personal responsibility and a well-developed conscience are the hallmarks of the "standard" that Lockheed Martin aspires to set. The document places a high level of responsibility on the individual employee—both for knowing the guidelines and for acting on them. In one sense, this is inevitable, as any corporate entity ultimately depends on the actions and integrity of each flesh-and-blood human being who works for it. Yet in another sense, the emphasis on personal responsibility is misleading, especially in an environment where teamwork, the rapid flow of information, and the powerful pressure of deadlines mean that many key decisions are by their nature collective and improvised, rather than individual and carefully deliberated. *Setting the Standard* implicitly describes the ethics of a corporation as the sum total of millions of decisions made by individual actors. This approach brings to light one truth about human enterprise, and it promotes a healthy sense of personal investment in the corporation's character. But the approach evades another truth about the nature of corporate life: Corporations make decisions in different ways from individuals, in a world where the rules are constantly changing. In the absence of a more rigorous process of self-examination, it is perfectly possible for an individual to "sleep soundly" and still participate in collective actions that violate the principles of ethics and fair play.

The Hour of Truth

Setting the Standard is the gospel for Lockheed Martin's ethics program; the annual ethics awareness training program, developed and overseen by Brian Sears, is the most far-reaching regular ethics activity of the corporation. Its goal is to use a single, flexible instrument so that all 130,000 employees of Lockheed Martin in the United States and around the world spend at least one hour per year discussing ethics in their workplace. The annual awareness program is the best and most comprehensive example of the way in which Lockheed Martin approaches ethics. It shows the corporate effort at its most inventive and creative, and it also demonstrates the quite deliberate limits of that effort.

The idea of an annual "ethics hour" is easy to caricature. What is so paltry a commitment of time, in the context of 2,000 or more hours a year devoted to improving the bottom line? It is obvious that sixty minutes of any activity carved out of an entire year is barely enough to raise a series of important issues, much less to discuss them in depth, and still less to instill the deep commitment necessary to implant right-minded thinking and behavior. In all fairness, however, Lockheed Martin officials describe the ethics awareness program as only the beginning of their effort, as a single common denominator on which a variety of other programs are based. There are plenty of institutions in American life that require no discussion whatsoever of ethics as a routine part of their employees' work. (I do not know of any university, for example, that requires every member of its community to engage in this kind of discussion.) An hour a year is a step that many of us have never taken.[4]

Furthermore, the challenge of developing a tool that works for people at every level of the corporation, of every type of job and temperament, and in every corner of the country and the world is no small one. Beginning with the development of the *Dilbert*-based "Ethics Challenge" in 1997, Lockheed Martin adopted the idea that it was not enough simply to expose employees to ethics awareness, but that it really *mattered* that they responded to it, even that they *liked* it. The program's success is measured not only by its effectiveness in reaching employees, but also by how positively they respond to it.

In the years since 1997, the ethics awareness program has developed a rhythm and a routine of its own, and it has developed and matured thematically since its first iteration. The program is redesigned each year with new cases, and every two years or so Sears and his team develop a new format, to keep it fresh and allow employees to explore new approaches. Steve Cohen, who found his way into the ethics world by owning the rights to *Dilbert,* has taken advantage of serendipity to become an all-seasons corporate ethics consultant as the principal of a new business, now called Ethics, Inc. He has remained a key player not only in the annual awareness training but also in a host of Lockheed Martin ethics and compliance programs.

Each winter, Sears, Cohen, and members of their respective teams gather in a series of meetings to map out the themes and process for the next year's training. Sears and the Lockheed ethics team identify the key topics they would like to emphasize, and they generate a list of new "cases" culled from the company records. Cohen and his team provide the pizzazz: educational strategies, a new format, some new graphics, a clever video, and an internal marketing campaign. By March, the materials are fully in production.

As with the original "Ethics Challenge," rollout begins with great fanfare in late April or early May, in the suite of the chief executive officer (CEO). The chief executive himself presides over the first formal session of the program, participating along with the top executives of the company. Each executive in turn leads the program with his or her senior staff, so between May and August the program "cascades" down through the corporation, with employees meeting in groups ranging from four to twenty-four, in conference rooms and offices in all of Lockheed Martin's facilities. Each employee duly signs the attendance sheet, completes the training, and most fill out an anonymous survey giving feedback to the designers. By the end of the summer, the bulk of the corporation has been through the training. Makeup sessions are held for those who missed out the first time around, and the ethics officers commence the hunt for the stragglers whom they call "onesies" and "twosies," especially Lockheed Martin employees who work off site or as consultants within other corporate settings. The training is intended for groups, but flexible enough for people to use it with a single partner, or even in a "solitaire" format.

The format has changed since 1997, but the basic principle of group discussion of real-life cases has remained intact. *Dilbert* and the "Ethics Challenge" lasted two years, until it was obvious that changing the color of the box would no longer make the concept seem fresh and new. The next format was called "Trust Building," followed by the "Ethics Daily," with a mock newspaper (yes, with a *Dilbert* strip) and a video featuring a well-known actor. When Lockheed Martin employees gathered in the spring and summer of 2003, they opened up a white box with stylized faces in bright colors adorning its cover. The 2003 Lockheed Martin Ethics Challenge was called "Perspectives."

With "Perspectives," the annual awareness training added a new twist: the idea that different individuals might have different points of view on a key decision. At the beginning of the training session, the leader divided the work group into three teams, generally with three to six employees on each team. After the introductory video with the pep talk from (now retired) CEO Vance Coffman and chief operating officer (COO) and now CEO Bob Stevens, the leader distributed a set of booklets to each team. As in previous years, the booklets contained a series of simplified real-life Lockheed Martin ethics situations, but this time each team's booklet presented the case from the "perspective" of one of the fictional characters in the case.

Case 24, for example, presents a situation where, after years of negotiating a tax dispute, Lockheed Martin receives a tax settlement from the Internal Revenue Service for $100 million. An account named Peter in Lockheed's tax office does his own calculation on the interest owed the corporation, and, lo and behold, he discovers that the IRS overpaid the company by $5 million. Peter tells his boss, Akeem, who notifies Todd, the corporation's point of contact at the IRS. Todd insists that the IRS calculation was correct, that there was no error, that Lockheed Martin does not have to return any money. What now is the right thing for Akeem to do?

Armed with their booklets, the teams meet in separate corners of the room to ponder the case. All three booklets have a general description of the situation, but Team A's booklet includes a more detailed version of Peter's side of the story. "I used to work for the IRS before I came to Lockheed Martin," Peter says, "so I'm fairly confident that my calculation is correct. . . . I just have to shake my head and wonder what's going on. We want to pay back $5 million, but the IRS doesn't want it?"

Team B looks at the situation from Todd's point of view. "With all due respect to Peter," says Todd, "I've been doing my job for fifteen years and I know how to calculate interest. . . . Even if I'm wrong, and I'm sure I'm not, the company still makes out. What's the big deal?"

The third team's booklet is marked "D" for decision maker, for the burden of addressing the situation falls upon the beleaguered Akeem, who is the tax department manager. Todd was "a little defensive," Akeem reflects, "and [he] reminded me of his 15 years with the agency. Okay, I respect that, but I also reviewed the details with Peter, and I believe we were overpaid by $5 million." Still, he has called the mistake to the attention of the IRS, and he has been rebuffed. Hasn't he already fulfilled his ethical obligation?

Teams discuss their cases for six or seven minutes, answering questions on a worksheet marked "Get in Character!" Employees are told in boldface to "**Answer the questions from your character's perspective, not your own.**" The groups tackle three questions: "Who are you and what do you care about or want?" "Which ethics principles are most relevant to this situation and why?" "What to you think the Decision Maker should do, and why?

These worksheets now serve as the "script" for one bold volunteer from each team, who must stand in front of the group and role play the character. The quality and intensity of these performances varies considerably. Some natural hams enjoy the chance to give their parts extra rhetorical flourishes. Some have a hard time stepping into the part of a character that they find exceptionally thick headed ("Who in their right mind would ever *offer* to give money back to the IRS?"). But most stumble through the part in an awkward third-person, too shy to play the role fully, too used to following instructions to abandon the format altogether. Still staying in character, team members are allowed to ask one another questions for a minute or two. "After a team presents," says the Leader's Guide, "encourage them with a simple acknowledgment such as 'Good job.'"

The idea is to help employees to envision ethics situations as dilemmas where two or more people might have conflicting interpretations. "Our interests influence our perspective," says the Leader's Guide, "and our perspective influences our opinion about what is right. That's why individuals may reach different conclusions even when they have considered the same factors. When confronted with a difficult decision, it's important to consider the perspectives of all involved. Your own perspective may change." Without saying so explicitly, the format cleverly opens up possibilities for conversation about the obstacles to "doing the right thing" in a competitive environment where ethics may be the number one "value" but profits are the number one measure of performance. Tax Refund's "Peter" cannot be sure that anyone—least of all his boss—will thank him for uncovering an error that may "cost" the corporation $5 million. For that matter, savvy discussants will point out that Todd's job at the IRS may be in jeopardy if he concedes that he has made an error of this magnitude. Akeem, as decision maker, may consult the "ethics principles," but he may also calculate how Peter and Todd's knowledge of the situation will affect him, should the facts become known at a later date.

Having batted things around from their own perspectives, the teams are finally permitted to step out of character and talk through the decision, based on the corporation's ethics principles. Here, however, the open-endedness of the format comes to an end. The group may come to one conclusion—or more than one—but the Leader's Guide finally shows the corporation's hand in the form of an "epilogue" in the words of the decision maker. Unsurprisingly, Akeem's decision in "Tax Refund" is to work around Todd and to call the problem to the attention of others at the IRS until the agency can see the mistake and take back the money. "The IRS was highly appreciative," Akeem reports, "and commended us on our honesty." In case the point was not clear enough, Akeem goes on to say that the next time the IRS *overbilled* the corporation, getting that problem fixed was a snap. This case was particularly satisfying, because it involved five of the corporation's six ethics principles—honesty, integrity, trust, responsibility, and citizenship—all at once.

The "Perspectives" cases follow this format, presenting characters who are earnest, dedicated Lockheed Martin employees, opening up some difficult and possibly even subversive questions, but then using the epilogues to tidy matters up and provide groups with a clear, company-approved line of reasoning.

Cases treat serious issues head-on, but in their mildest possible form. Case 19 is the only 2003 case to address the issue of "harassment." There's no physical action or direct pressure from a boss in Case 19; the issue, instead, involves a middle manager named Sam, a year from retirement, who tells Vanessa, a security guard in the lobby of his building, how sexy she looks in her uniform. "I know you're supposed to be politically correct these days, but what do you want from me?" Sam asks in his "perspective." "I've got three grandchildren—you think I'm some kind of harasser? Is she going to make a federal case out of this and screw up my last year?" Sam's joking is witnessed by a receptionist named Irene, who sympathizes with Vanessa, but in this case, the "Decision Maker" is Vanessa herself, who has to decide how far to take things. "I really don't like being teased about my looks every morning by Sam," she says. "I know he's been around a long time, but what gives him the right to say all that stuff in front of other people?"

In the end, Vanessa's decision, as presented in the Leader's Guide, is no more elaborate than just to talk to Sam. "At first he was really defensive, talking about how people needed to lighten up. But as I explained how uncomfortable he made me feel with his comments, he apologized." Here, as in many of the other cases, the company presents ethics problems as no more than a matter of miscommunication. As the company's "principles" suggest that ethics and openness go hand in hand, the message is reinforced in the awareness cases; problems vanish as open dialogue leads to mutual understanding.

Most of the cases present low-level, low-stakes situations that average employees are likely to face on a day-to-day basis. The strategy makes sense for a corporation-wide program, since cases have to look at least somewhat familiar to the vast majority of employees, but the overall effect is also to reduce ethics to a series of modest human relations problems. In Case 10, a supervisor named Paul has scruples about signing expense reports for a staff engineer named Jean, who has to travel frequently; better communication is the answer. In Case 17, a computer technician named Jeff decides that he has to warn his coworker Dan against letting a subcontractor named Aaron pick up the tab at happy hour. When a manager named Martha in Case 27 asks Roger to work overtime to meet a deadline on the very night when Roger's daughter has a piano recital, the two of them talk and work out a compromise where Roger can go to the recital and come back to the office and finish up afterward. While employees are encouraged to work things out among themselves, the Leader's Guide also reminds them frequently that the company resources of the Ethics Office, the General Counsel, and Human Resources are there to back them up if all else fails.

Very rarely, a case ventures farther afield, touching not only on personal decision making but also on the larger question of the corporation's ethical position in the world. Case 16 addresses the Foreign Corrupt Practices Act (FCPA) by describing the tense political environment in the fictional country of Asean, where Lockheed Martin's offices have been the target of protests by "radical anti-American activists." An expatriate employee named Yung has been offering snacks to the police officers assigned to guard the building, on the advice of Min, an office manager who is hired locally. Min has also suggested that cash payments to the higher ranking officers "as a sign of appreciation for service above and beyond their normal duties" is customary. "We are guests in this country," Yung says, "and we should respect local customs."

The case threatens to open up a host of complicated ethical questions involving the role of an American corporation in a developing country and the place of the weapons industry in the global marketplace. What is the proper relationship between a wealthy American corporation and an impoverished local population? To what extent does Lockheed Martin act as an extension of the U.S. government and its interests when operating abroad? What direct and indirect influences does the presence of the corporation bring to bear on local politics and social change? These possible "perspectives" however, are neatly sidestepped in Case 19, to make room for the narrower and more practical question of whether providing courtesies to the local constabulary violates U.S. law. "Yes, the officers are considered 'foreign officials,'" argues the local office manager, Min, "but none of them are in a position to influence the government officials who are involved in purchasing products from Lockheed Martin. I am worried that if we don't make these payments the police may decide not to show up one day when we really need them." In the end, Howard, the regional director checks with counsel. The lawyers approve the snacks and meals, but they nix the cash payments. A coda suggests that a donation to the police benevolent fund would be allowed under the FCPA, if given prior approval.

Lockheed Martin's ethics office prides itself on a spirit of continuous self-improvement. In 2004, Brian Sears led a thoroughgoing redesign that reconsidered the basic theme of the awareness training. "Perspectives" gave way to a program called "The Ethics Effect," which focuses on the larger impact of decisions that involve the application of ethical principles. An "ethics meter" provides a visual aid for a series of choices that range from "unethical" and "on thin ice" at one end to "ethically sound" or "highly ethical" at the positive end of the spectrum. Another innovation this year involved including cases "pulled from the headlines"—slightly disguised accounts of national stories like the 2003 scandals at Boeing.

I sat in with Brian Sears on one of the first training sessions in 2004, for a group of managers in the Integrated Systems & Solutions facility in

Gaithersburg, Maryland. Sears enjoys watching how the case discussions play out in real life, and he is always surprised by the debates and interpretations that surface. In the session that I attend, a dozen managers have a lively discussion about Case 3, in which an acting manager named Bill has to figure out what to do when he suspects that some of the travel expenses reported by a coworker named Jim are fictitious. Some of the choices are easy. "Approved it, but told Jim that he expects a favor in return" is a slam dunk for "unethical," and the group agrees that "Waited for a permanent manager to be announced and let him or her deal with it" is ducking the issue and thereby skating "on thin ice." But they debate over which solution is better: asking Jim directly for an explanation of the questioned expenses, or simply turning things over to the audit department. (The approved answer prefers confronting Jim directly and giving him a chance to explain himself, before turning him over to the jaws of the bureaucracy.)

Sears fields criticism from some of the members of the training session over one of the proposed solutions in Case 2, which addresses issues of environment, safety, and health. A manager named Janet discovers that members of her team have begun to develop severe allergies in their temporary work space, and she has to figure out how to balance employee health with company policy. One of the proposed choices is for Janet to purchase allergy medicine herself and dispense it to her team. The booklet terms this a "gray area" solution, tending toward the ethical because it shows Janet's personal concern for her staff, but tending toward the unethical because it ignores the source of the problem. In the training session, however, an irate participant complains that this is the worst solution of all—after all, she complains, Janet is no physician, and she might well be doing more harm than good to her staff by pushing over-the-counter medicine on them. Sears takes diligent notes, and then offers a *mea culpa* to the group at the end of the session. "You know, all the hours that we spent working on that case, and we just never thought of it in that light," he confesses. "That's why I love coming to these sessions— you just learn new things every time."

Reflecting the language and tone of *Setting the Standard,* the annual ethics awareness training makes personal responsibility and open communication its hallmarks. Ethics problems are sliced and shaped into a series of moments of individual decision making, and problems are resolved by bringing the facts and perspectives into the light. The program is a triumph in its dynamic engagement of thousands of employees. It is equally ingenious in restricting the scope of ethics problems, and bolstering the corporation's self-image as a collective enterprise of decent, hard-working folk.

Beyond Awareness

The annual awareness program is the single largest ethics program to come out of company headquarters over the course of a year, but it is only the entering wedge of an extensive host of programs intended both to meet the concerns of federal regulators, and to "market" ethics as a value more extensively throughout the corporation.

Fundamental to the overall effort is the corporation's extensive compliance program. "Compliance" in the defense industry environment means, quite simply, knowing and following the applicable law, usually the laws and regulations of the U.S. government. The ethics staff likes to think of compliance as an essential bedrock for a more comprehensive program: "It is important to train employees on what is *required,* as it cultivates doing what is *right*." Everyone needs to know and understand the relevant law; from that foundation, you can, they claim, build a values-based culture where employees not only follow the letter of the law, but follow a spirit of "doing the right thing" in situations where the law is vague or unhelpful.

The compliance office develops training modules on thirty different topics, ranging from antitrust law to insider trading to protecting classified information. Employees must "pass" the compliance modules in areas relevant to their work; the most senior executives have to take them all. Between 1995 and 2003, Lockheed Martin employees completed nearly 2.5 million compliance training sessions. By far the bulk of these sessions are now done online, at the employee's convenience, in modules that take less than an hour. Steve Cohen has expanded his repertoire beyond the annual ethics awareness program to help develop some of these modules, which simulate and parody movie genres like horror and mystery to lighten up what could otherwise be a deadly process. Company executives like to zip through the modules on the airplane, punching in the answers on their Palm Pilots. The compliance office keeps careful track of the corporation by business area and company, monitoring closely which units have run their employees through the relevant trainings and which are lagging behind. The statistics are not just kept from a sense of order; they are also crucial documentation, in the event that something goes wrong, for the company to indemnify itself against the charge that it was negligent in its duty to inform its employees of the contours of the law.

Brian Sears sees compliance and awareness as necessary, but not sufficient. For several years he had been pondering ways to encourage Lockheed Martin employees to invest more personally in the idea of ethics in the corporation. In 2003, he introduced the first annual Lockheed Martin Ethics Film Festival. Sears put out a call throughout the company for employees to make short films that would illustrate the importance of Lockheed Martin's values in the workplace. The films could take any form, and address any topic related to company values, but employees had to make the films on their own time and at their own expense. The incentive? The makers of the three top entries would be invited to the ethics officers' conference in Orlando, where the winning entry would be announced at the closing banquet.

Somewhat to Sears's surprise, the first Lockheed Martin Ethics Film Festival attracted twenty entries, involving the combined efforts of dozens of employees from coast to coast, with an entry from across the border in Canada as well. Most of the entries painted tongue-in-cheek portraits of employee hijinks: back-room poker games; the employee who coughs into the phone while calling in sick so he can watch a big football game on television; wads of money changing hands in shady deals.

At the Orlando banquet, the finalists show up decked out in their finest. There are the obligatory jokes about the red carpet and the paparazzi, as they work their way through the meal and wait for the big announcement. After dinner, four fire safety specialists from the Space Systems operation in Houston sing the barbershop quartet number that was the centerpiece of their film, "Harmony of Ethics." ("*Speak* truth with *Cour*-age / *Do* what you *prom*-ise / *Be*-have responsib-*ly* . . . .")

Walter Osadciw, an engineer from the Integrated Systems & Solutions division in Syracuse, New York, attends the conference with his sixth-grade daughter, who plays a starring role in his film, "Setting the Example." Osadciw himself appears in the film as a red-eyed, harassed executive, working at home on the afternoon before a big presentation, who with a few taps on the keyboard changes the numbers on his spreadsheet from losses to profits. Meanwhile, next door at the kitchen table, Walter's daughter is busy altering her report card to bring a set of "C" grades into the "B" range. The message flashes up on the screen at the film's end: "It's not just what you're doing . . . It's what you're teaching."

James Houghtaling, also from Syracuse, regales his table with the finer points of claymation, the technique he used in his entry. His "Ethics Infomercial" features a buyer who snores noisily in his office, where the walls are emblazoned with posters extolling the Lockheed Martin values. The buyer wakes up only to accept a gift of cash from a supplier and check out pornographic web sites ("Clay Girl"!!!). "Ethics: We help you sleep at night," is Houghtaling's tag line. With suitable fanfare, the envelope is produced after dinner. The "Ethics Infomercial" is declared the winner, and James Houghtaling walks away with Lockheed Martin's first ethics "Oscar."

Brian Sears is thrilled with the results of the film festival. "When I first proposed this, I really didn't have any idea whether we'd get any entries at all," he confesses later. "But I think this shows how much enthusiasm there is in the company for the kinds of things we're trying to do with our ethics program. People did this on their own time, and look what they came up with." The film festival is now enshrined as one of the corporate ethics office's annual rituals.

In a similar vein, the ethics office has established an annual "Chairman's Award" for a Lockheed Martin employee who has performed some ethically upright action in the previous year. The first winner, selected in 2002, was Ron Covais, a vice-president in the business development area. Working on a deal with a foreign entity, Covais blew the whistle on an "inappropriate request for payment by an individual representing the customer," instigating both an internal and a U.S. government investigation. The next year, Vic La Rosa in systems integration inadvertently received an e-mail from a government source with technical details about a competitor's product; he deleted the e-mail, and reported the situation to the sender. The Chairman's Award sends the message to employees at large that they will be rewarded for risk-taking conduct that follows the company's values.

Measuring Success

"One of the things about the ethics business: you can't grade people," says Phil Tenney, director of ethics operations. "But we're an engineering company. We need metrics for everything, to see if things are going well." Tenney is the man entrusted with the responsibility of measuring the success of Lockheed Martin's ethics program. His principal tool is a biennial survey of the corporation's entire workforce, which he puts together with the help of the Ethics Resource Center, a nonprofit group based in Washington, D.C., that consults to dozens of corporations.

In 2001, nearly half of Lockheed Martin's employees returned the surveys, so Phil Tenney had more than 60,000 responses to deal with. (Actually, the surveys were administered by and returned to the Ethics Resource Center, to assure the integrity of the process. But Tenney spent a couple of days on a lawn chair in the summer of 2001 working his way through the many thousands of individual comments that supplemented the multiple-choice questions.) The vast majority of the surveys were completed online, although more than 7,000 were filled out by hand. When Lockheed Martin conducted the corporation's first survey in 1995, barely a quarter of them were returned.

The trendlines on the survey over the past several years are gratifying for Tenney and his colleagues in the Office of Ethics and Business Conduct. Nearly all employees (98 percent) asserted that they know what ethical business conduct is, and 95 percent were clear about how to find advice about ethics issues in the workplace. Even better, every time the survey has been done, a higher percentage of employees believes that Lockheed's ethical principles are applied always or often in the everyday work of the corporation. Seventy-four percent felt that they always or often felt that "honesty" was evident at Lockheed Martin in 1997; that figure had climbed to 86 percent by 2001 (and the number that believed that honesty was "never" in evidence had shrunk to a fraction of 1 percent). The figures for the other ethics principles have showed similar jumps.

When the survey moves from abstract principles to specific observations, however, the picture is somewhat less rosy. The percentage that occasionally or frequently felt pressured by fellow employees or management to compromise Lockheed Martin's standards was down in 2001, but the figure still stood at 12 percent. Those who felt such pressure cited aggressive business objectives, schedule pressures, and overbearing supervisors as the principal causes. The survey does not bother to ask whether employees have themselves engaged in unethical conduct, under the sound reasoning that answers to this question might be something less than reliable.

Most troubling to the corporation's ethics leadership were results that showed that misbehavior could be observed but go unreported. Thirty percent of the company's employees in 2001 said that they occasionally or frequently observed conduct that they believed violated Lockheed Martin's ethics standards. Since, as we have seen, the standards cover a variety of minor matters as well as major misconduct, this figure alone is not particularly shocking, given the variety of human experience and behavior in the workplace. Of more concern, however, was the chart that shows that of those who saw things amiss, fewer than half (43 percent) reported the conduct.[5] Those who failed to report simply did not trust the Lockheed Martin system; they explained their reluctance by cynicism (more than half simply did not believe that anything would be done) or by fear of retaliation of management. In a work environment with tens of thousands of unionized line employees, as well as engineers and former military personnel, it has proved difficult to persuade Lockheed Martin employees that reporting ethics concerns is a higher good than loyalty to one's peers. Fear of retaliation by management decreased (among the whole workforce, from 27 percent in 1999 to 16 percent in 2001), but the figure remained an indicator of a lingering culture of mistrust.

The Office of Ethics and Business conduct used the results of the 2001 survey to craft new responses to a specific problem: the capacity of supervisors to address ethics issues. The survey showed a high level of disappointment among those employees who did report ethics misconduct to their supervisors. The response was often ineffectual; indeed, some employees felt that their supervisors failed to recognize when an ethics issue was in front of them. In response, the corporate office launched a new initiative in 2002 called "Ethics Tools for Leaders," designed to reach the corporation's 15,000 managers and encourage them to be active participants in the company's ethics policies and process.

The 2001 survey presented an upbeat picture of employee "buy-in" to the corporation's abstract ethics principles, somewhat undercut by a streak of cynicism about Lockheed Martin's follow-through and questions about the company's commitment to its own workforce. More than one-third of the respondents could not say affirmatively that they felt valued as an employee of the corporation. The evidence suggests that the ethics program has, in fact, contributed to employee goodwill, but that a strong minority of employees still wonder just how deep the corporation's commitment really goes. [6]

On the Front Lines

The people responsible for defining and maintaining that sense of commitment are Lockheed Martin's sixty-five ethics officers. "You must be honest, trustworthy, independent, discreet, and responsible," says the corporation's Ethics Officer Resource Manual. "More importantly, you must be perceived as such by the employee population."

In an era of intensive scrutiny, the figure of the "ethics officer" has been an increasingly visible presence in American corporations. Part counselor, part investigator, part marketer, the ethics officer is intended to serve as the living emblem of the corporation's principles.

No one enters Lockheed Martin on the ethics officer job track. It is a standing principle that ethics officers should be chosen from among the ranks, by identifying veteran employees who know the company culture and have demonstrated loyalty over time. There is indeed a national Ethics Officers Association, based in Massachusetts, with more than 1,000 members as of 2004.[7] But the idea that ethics officers represent a new, mobile professional group would be anathema to the Lockheed Martin culture. Ethics in the Lockheed Martin conception is only partly about universal principles of the right and the good. It is much more about strengthening commonsense ideas that the corporation likes to think of as homegrown.

Lockheed Martin employees most typically become ethics officers through other service offices. Brian Sears at corporate headquarters was an auditor. Alice Edmonds at Lockheed Martin Space Operations in Crystal City, Virginia, had spent nearly three decades in human resources, before moving into an ethics officer position. Cathy Harris, in Fairfax, Virginia, is a relative oddity: An engineer and a program manager by background, she chose to become an ethics officer because she realized that "the farther I went up the management chain, the farther I was getting away from the people issues that I cared about most." Vice-president Maryanne Lavan would like to see more employees do a stint as ethics officers as they rise within the corporate hierarchy: "I'd like the ethics office to be a place for high-potential employees," she says. "It's good experience for people on the rise. You should know what people are upset about and complain about, and you can't know until you're in the middle of it."

"People issues" are obvious drivers for Lockheed Martin ethics officers. Gregarious, sincere, slightly self-deprecating, they spend a lot of their time providing informal advice and counseling to employees, as well as troubleshooting minor problems. Working in relative isolation from one another, they have considerable opportunity to be responsive to Lockheed Martin's rank and file, operating without the stigma that is sometimes attached to offices like human resources or the general counsel, which are often, fairly or not, perceived as looking after the interests of management first. Their first job is to be visible: When you walk the halls of the Integrated Systems & Solutions facility in Gaithersberg, Maryland, you cannot avoid Wendy Donaldson's amiable face, beaming out at you from every bulletin board. Since Donaldson's area of responsibility includes Lockheed Martin units around the country, and as distant as California, she has established a drop-in program she calls "The Ethics Officer is IN" to highlight her availability whenever she is on site. Ethics officers are encouraged to "Be Accessible," "Be Visible," and "Build Trust and Communication." Some conduct informal ethics discussion sessions, but most carry on this part of their work in conversations in cubicles, over coffee, and in any place where employees might sit down for a break.

While selling the corporation's values person by person is an important element of the ethics officer's job, the most sustained and complex part of the work is more adversarial: the process of formal ethics investigations. Since the implementation of the federal sentencing guidelines, a rock-bottom fundamental aspect of any corporate ethics program has been the establishment of a confidential "hot line" where employees can report unethical or illegal behavior that they observe while on the job.

At Lockheed Martin, there are dozens of such hotlines, known as "Helplines." Many ethics officers have established one within their business areas, so employees feel that they can report their complaints to someone who has at least some knowledge of local conditions. Often this line is answered only by the ethics officer. Company policy instructs the ethics officers to tell callers that they may remain anonymous if they so choose (caller ID is not permitted on these lines), but it also instructs them to encourage callers to provide their identity to the ethics officer, who is pledged not to reveal the identity unless legally bound to do so.

If employees decide, for whatever reason, that they do not wish to call their local hotline, Lockheed Martin maintains a company-wide ethics Helpline at 1–800-[LM ETHICS]. The man who usually picks up calls to that number is Bud Reid, a thirty-year veteran of the U.S. Army who moved into the private sector in the 1980s, accepting a position with Martin Marietta. Reid had been in communications and public relations in the Army, and soon after his arrival at Martin Marietta he was persuaded to join the team that was developing the company's new ethics program. Reid still believes that some of the best aspects of Lockheed Martin's ethics operation—its strong centralization, its innovations in terms of "marketing" ethics, and its emphasis on networking—grew more out of the Martin Marietta heritage than the Lockheed side.

Bud Reid estimates that he takes between fifty and sixty calls per week on the ethics Helpline. Many of the calls are human-resource and bureaucratic matters: An employee feels slighted by his supervisor; an employee feels that she has not received the appropriate benefits. Some are calls for advice: Can I take a subcontractor out to dinner? Is it okay if my daughter's marketing company solicits business from Lockheed Martin? Most of these contacts (two-thirds) end up as "memos to file," simply recording the fact of the call in the database, with no further action required. Reid takes even the smallest inquiry seriously, even if on the face of it the query has little to do with ethics. "Employees at the lower end of the food chain don't have much power," he says. "We see ourselves as advocates for the little guy. We want to work small cases just as hard as we can, so when the big ticket items come up, everyone has confidence in the system." "Memos to file" are a mark of success in the corporate ethics office; they suggest employee interest in and commitment to ethics, but at a level of seriousness that does not pose any significant threat.

Those cases that turn into investigations undergo, in theory at least, a rigorous twenty-one-step process that includes securing evidence, conferring with the legal office, conducting interviews, writing reports, having the matter reviewed by a supervisor, and recording every step in a database called CERTS. The ethics staff takes great pride and pleasure in this process; it is clear that there are few joys in ethics work that compare to "peeling back the onion," as Brian Sears and others like to say. The written procedure is elaborate and thorough, diagrammed with boxes of different shapes and sizes, arrows guiding the investigator through various possibilities of the narrative. If all goes well, the process ends with "Final Report Submitted," and if the "Decision Maker Accept" box follows the "YES" arrow, the satisfying conclusion is given as "Documentation Retention." After that, the process is in the hands of Human Resources or the legal department, which takes the appropriate action if the investigator has convincingly uncovered misdeeds.

Investigations are sometimes conducted in tandem with other units. In Gaithersberg, Maryland, I met with Judith Casey, the head of the Computer Incident Response Team (CIRT), and the three young college graduates whom she proudly calls her "boys." Casey, a twenty-year company veteran whose specialty used to be disaster recovery, moved into investigations, under the auspices of the company's security office. Now, she and "the boys"—Andrew Robbins, Johnny Perera, and Sam Maxwell—roam through the company's computer networks, keeping an eye out for employees who use their machines for personal use, or, more seriously, violate security or proprietary procedures. They work closely on investigations with Wendy Donaldson, the ethics officer on site, and they bring to their work an ambivalent zealousness that reflects the conflicting values of the high-tech world. On the one hand, they are a little sheepish about their role as company spies—"It's easy to slip into a God complex," says Sam Maxwell. But on the other hand, they feel themselves working at ground zero of corporate reform, and they take employee misdeeds personally. Andrew Robbins was studying computer science at the University of Virginia when the corporate scandals broke in 2000 and 2001; now he says that "the best neighbor is a nosy neighbor," something he remembers as he snoops through suspicious files. After all, says

Johnny Perera, "The monitoring is open. It's very clear from day one that your privacy is not protected on the Lockheed Martin computer network." In an average year, Wendy Donaldson works a dozen or more cases with the CIRT, with the majority ending in some sort of consequence for one or more employees.

Lockheed Martin's ethics officers cheerfully acknowledge that minor, even trivial cases are a large part of their caseload. "We're something like an internal affairs division in a police department," ethics officer Roger Kingman explains to me. "We don't frequently deal with the kinds of things that bring down an Enron." He agrees to walk me through a typical investigation, as long as I do not mention his real name or location, and as long as I change some of the details about the case: Protection, as far as possible, for both the accuser and the accused in an investigation is a fundamental principle.

Roger Kingman generally conducts only three or four investigations each year himself. More often, he will refer cases that require investigation to the security department, or to Human Resources, or to the general counsel; he will then monitor those cases, and advise on particular aspects, but he will not play a leading role. He is not prepared to handle what he calls "cloak-and-dagger" stuff (for example, surreptitiously trailing an employee who is alleged to be conducting an outside business on company time), nor can he pursue arcane questions of financial or technical misdoing. But certain situations are a match for his skills and his schedule, or else they involve suspicions about the performance of one of the other investigating offices themselves, so he will take a more prominent role.

One day in the winter of 2003, an employee named Anne came to visit Roger. On the job for less than a year, Anne felt that she was underutilized and badly treated by her supervisor, Beth. Anne had previously complained up the ladder to Beth's manager, to Human Resources, and even to the company president, but she had received no satisfaction. A coworker had suggested that she take her complaint to the ethics officer, so that is why she appeared one day in Kingman's office. Anne asked Kingman to help her out, and she asked him, incidentally, whether he was aware that Beth had the good fortune of having her own mother, Carol, as her supervisor, even though they did not work at the same location. Is that kind of thing allowed at Lockheed Martin? Anne asked.

Kingman started nosing around, trying to find out what he could about Anne's assertions without confronting Beth and Carol directly. "You'd be surprised," he told me, "how difficult it is to get information in a company this big, with all the changes in organizational structure and management." He found out that few people had much sympathy for Anne, who was not considered an outstanding worker and had a reputation for being a bit of a whiner. His inquiries about Beth and Carol, however, turned up some surprises. The two women had different last names, but indeed, Carol was Beth's mother. It turned out that Carol, who was responsible for helping the communications division hire contract employees, had shoehorned Beth into her first job at Lockheed Martin, and then had maneuvered things so that Beth received a hefty raise in her first year. Carol did not exactly hide the fact that Beth was her daughter, but she implied to everyone who asked that the arrangement had been approved by someone higher up the chain. Kingman learned that within a few months, Carol was even the person who was formally approving her daughter's time sheets.

Now Anne's original complaint was somewhat beside the point. Kingman confronted Carol about the situation, and discovered that she did not believe that she had done anything wrong. Her daughter Beth, after all, was widely acknowledged as an excellent employee, and she felt that she had been sufficiently open about her relationship with others in the corporation. Carol admitted that there were elements of the situation (Beth's spiraling salary, Carol's oversight of Beth's time sheets) that perhaps "didn't look good," but she viewed these as superficial problems. "Towards the end of the conversation I spotted some crocodile tears," Kingman says, but by that point he did not have a great deal of confidence in Carol's sincerity. He brought the facts of the case to a committee of senior executives; in short order, Beth was terminated because her hiring was tainted from the beginning, and Carol, a thirty-year Lockheed Martin employee, was also let go. "When I tell people what I do for a living, they think I'm helping people deal with ethical dilemmas all day long," Kingman says. "In fact, a lot of what I do is to figure out whether what people did was or was not in violation of company policy."

Indeed, the ethics officers view the fact that so many cases are trivial as a sign of success—like the small-town cop who can give more traffic tickets because no dead bodies ever turn up on Main Street. Many calls like the one to Kingman reflect human resource problems—an employee claims that she has been passed up for promotion, or her supervisor is spending too much time on the golf course. One of Brian Sears's favorite cases involves the employee who called the ethics hotline to complain that "I ain't dead." Sears's investigation revealed that the woman's benefits had been cut off, because she had been mixed up with another employee by the same name who had indeed died in the previous month. As Bud Reid says, any complaint that an employee *believes* is an ethics issue should be treated as an ethics issue. This is the way that ethics becomes instilled and trusted throughout the company culture.

Ethics officers are particularly concerned, they say, about the vulnerability of Lockheed Martin's newest employees to misdeeds. Some of this is a matter of opportunity; in many Lockheed Martin facilities, new employees must wait for months with little to do before receiving their security clearances to work on sensitive projects. In the meantime, boredom provides the temptation to stray, especially with regard to computer use. Some of this vulnerability is ascribed to generational change—a perceived lack of moral fiber in younger people, and the lack of a clear moral framework for the Internet and other aspects of the high-tech world of the twenty-first century. The ethics office assumes some of the responsibility itself. Noting that survey results showed that new employees were frequently confused and underinformed about the corporation's values, they created a new "ethics orientation" to bring new hires up to speed. Ethics officers are quite open about the continuing problems with the newest members of the Lockheed Martin family, but new employees, with restricted access to information and equipment, are seldom in a position to cause deep and lasting harm through their peccadilloes.

It is much more difficult, however, to persuade the ethics staff to talk about more serious cases. When I ask about investigations of significant breaches, I hear stories like the one about the former employee in Fairfax, Virginia, who managed to run up thousands of dollars in personal travel and other expenses on a corporate credit card, before he was caught through a routine company-wide audit. Brian Sears does not pretend that Lockheed Martin is spotless at the upper end of the "food chain," but he is unwilling to give me a sense of the scope and frequency of investigations of senior management. In the absence of more specific data, it is difficult to escape the suspicion that a very great amount of the corporation's ethics assets are devoted to the mundane. It is difficult to see how investigations of golf games and performance reviews can genuinely put a stop to the kinds of high-level corporate scandals that have infected some of the biggest names of industry in recent years.

Cooperation Among Competitors

Lockheed Martin's ethics program does not operate in a vacuum. Indeed, it is part of an unusually active and cooperative arrangement between other defense contractors that aims to establish ethics as firmly as possible through the industry. The Defense Industry Initiative on Ethics and Business Conduct (DII) is an unusual consortium. It has no dedicated staff and no office. What it has instead is a set of principles, and a steering committee composed of leading executives from the more than fifty defense contractors who have pledged to abide by those principles. The DII's principal activity is an annual conference in Washington, D.C., where companies share "best practices" in ethics. Its programs are coordinated by Richard Bednar, an attorney at the Washington, D.C., law firm of Crowell and Moring. Bednar serves not only as a hub of the network, but also as an active advocate for the member corporations in assuring the Department of Defense that its suppliers are maintaining high standards of integrity.

"In another milieu, these companies are vigorous competitors," Bednar says, "but in our milieu they cooperate in a way that is not replicated anywhere else." Bednar cites Lockheed Martin as a leader in the DII—both Lockheed and Martin Marietta were among the original signatories in 1986—but he is also quick to point out what he considers the wealth of creativity and sincerity throughout the industry. "This is a consortium that is populated with realists," he says. "These people know that trouble and unwanted conduct is going to come to any large corporation. The real question is: What are you going to do about it? Our members are willing to deal with root causes."

Like Lockheed Martin, other corporations in the industry have moved to "market" ethics more effectively within their organizations. Public relations campaigns, web-based modules, leveraging of company resources, widespread training sessions—the DII forum has helped companies build programs that make ethics highly visible within the corporation. Most observers agree that, largely because of the existence of the DII since the 1980s, many defense contractors had already created programs to address most of the recently enacted standards, even before the requirements of recent federal legislation.

Yet despite the success of the DII and the widespread adoption of ethics programs in the industry, one of its most important members was rocked by two enormous scandals in 2003. These incidents, involving the Boeing Corporation, left ethics officers across the defense industry wondering what went wrong, and just how vulnerable their own organizations might be to similar problems.

The two scandals at Boeing involved very different types of incidents. The first, coincidentally, involved Lockheed Martin. In 1998, Boeing was bidding for a new Air Force contract to build an "Evolved Expendable Launch Vehicle" (EELV), a launcher for military payloads. Lockheed Martin was bidding for the contract as well, but Boeing had an advantage: A former employee of Lockheed Martin had been hired by McDonnell-Douglas just prior to its merger with Boeing, and the employee had brought with him boxloads of documents related to Lockheed Martin's bid. The transfer of these technical and financial materials, proprietary information that belonged legally to Lockheed Martin, could have given Boeing a substantial advantage in framing a competitive bid for the contract. Boeing was in fact awarded the lion's share of the EELV business in 1998, but information about the existence of the proprietary information began to leak out the next year. Boeing tried to contain the damage by acknowledging the existence of a small number of documents in 1999, and by subsequently firing three of the employees involved. But wider allegations continued to surface, and by April 2003, under pressure of a grand jury subpoena and a federal investigation, Boeing had returned more than 25,000 pages of documents to Lockheed Martin. The EELV incident, in combination with two other documented incidents where Boeing illegally obtained proprietary information in connection with other contracts, prompted the Air Force to disqualify Boeing in July 2003 from three major projects, costing the corporation an estimated $5 billion in new business.

The second incident, which came to light later in 2003, was no less dramatic. In January 2003, Boeing hired Darleen Druyun as vice-president and deputy general manager of its Missile Defense Systems unit. Ms. Druyun had retired just two months earlier from a senior position in the U.S. Air Force, where her principal responsibilities were in the area of procurement. Following allegations by watchdog groups, the Department of Defense launched an investigation into the circumstances regarding Ms. Druyun's employment at Boeing, and the corporation subsequently undertook its own investigation. The company's investigation revealed that Boeing chief financial officer (CFO) Michael Sears had begun employment negotiations with Darleen Druyun not only while she was still with the Air Force, but at a time when she had responsibility for procurement matters in which Boeing was directly involved. On November 24, 2003, Boeing announced that both Sears and Druyun had been fired. A week later, to the consternation of the industry, Boeing CEO Philip Condit abruptly resigned. Within a year, two major scandals had cost a founding member of the DII not only billions of dollars of business, but also the jobs of its top leadership.

What went wrong? As at Lockheed Martin, Boeing had invested a great deal of time and money since 1986 in developing an extensive ethics and business conduct program. (Indeed, Nancy Higgins, who headed Lockheed Martin's program from 2001 to 2003, had previously led the Boeing operation for several years.) So how had such dramatic and costly incidents happened? In the aftermath of each scandal, Boeing sought outside help to answer these questions. Former U.S. Senator Warren Rudman and a team from the New York law firm of Paul, Weiss, Rifkind, Wharton & Garrison prepared extensive reports on each situation.[8] Rudman's reports were generally positive about the extent and seriousness of Boeing's ethics program, applauding the corporation for its long-standing commitment and for its allocation of resources. The reports called both the EELV and Druyun incidents isolated events. Nevertheless, the reports made a series of recommendations, including more direct involvement by senior management, more resources for the ethics program, and more training on specific topics. The reports also highlighted the relatively decentralized structure of Boeing's ethics program. Boeing's program left considerable autonomy to the individual business units, creating inconsistencies and variations across the larger corporation. The corporation's "Ethics Advisors" reported directly to their company presidents, with only a "dotted-line" report to the vice-president for business ethics, thereby creating questions about their genuine independence.

Lockheed Martin could take some comfort in the Rudman reports' argument about centralization. Its own ethics program clearly has a strong foundation at corporate headquarters; while it also wrestles with the complexities of units with dozens of different "heritages," creating consistency across the corporation has been a significant element of the program for many years. Yet despite the reassurances of the Rudman reports, the scandals at Boeing are deeply troubling. While there are important variations, the DII has helped assure that there are a great many similarities between the ethics programs of the major defense contractors. If two scandals with such major consequences could emerge in a single year in a corporation where ethics had been on the agenda for some time, then perhaps the weaknesses are more significant than they first appear. It is possible that Boeing's troubles stemmed from a combination of bad luck and a few small defects in an otherwise healthy structure. But it is also possible that the very extensiveness of the ethics programs offered by DII signatories masks some serious vulnerabilities that have not yet been fully confronted.

Accomplishments

"One Company, One Team": This is the mantra that I hear at the ethics officers' conference, and after a while, I come to realize that corporate harmonization may be the single most important function of Lockheed Martin's ethics operation. The top executives have begun to understand that diversity—defined in a peculiarly broad way—is one of the most significant challenges facing the corporation in the coming years. The ethics program aspires to create a shared rhetoric that binds a far-flung set of employees into a loyal and coherent body.

At the 2003 Orlando conference, Kimberly Galavetz, a vice-president in the audit division, shows up to speak on this topic. Galavetz is part of a leadership group that is tackling a company-wide initiative on diversity. The presenting problem, she explains, is the aging employee base of the company. More than 70 percent of Lockheed Martin's workforce is over forty, and with the prospect of a continuing buildup of the defense industry in the post-9/11 world, the corporation is likely to be doing a great deal of hiring in the coming decade. Lockheed Martin will need engineers and supporting staff by the thousands, and the next generation is not going to look like the current workforce. "Do we have a diverse enough employee population to think about the defense needs of this country in the years to come?" Galavetz asks rhetorically. "We have to admit that our customers in most cases are more diverse than we are." The message, as Galavetz expounds it, is clear. If ethics has been a success as a corporation-wide effort, then "diversity is the next foundational thing that we need to get baked in" to the corporate culture.

But what does diversity mean in the Lockheed Martin context? Galavetz is eager to expand the definition as broadly as possible, in order to avoid talking about any specific effort or problem. She manages to speak on diversity for nearly an hour without uttering the word "race." She mentions no specific racial, religious, or ethnic group. The words "affirmative action" and "multiculturalism" never cross her lips. Instead, diversity in Galavetz's exposition is a matter of style, of civility, of corporate identity. "Diversity at Lockheed Martin," she tells the group, "means creating an inclusive team that values and leverages each person's individuality." This means things like creating a "welcoming environment," promoting the idea that "we value each other across the corporation," and developing "good listening" and "flexible attitudes." Later, over lunch, she explains to me that not mentioning race is precisely the point. "We're trying to focus on diversity in *all* of its senses," she tells me, "not just focus on one aspect of it." Diversity at Lockheed Martin, in other words, means promoting a generalized aura of goodwill, and avoiding direct confrontation with any specific issues that might be threatening or divisive.

It is no coincidence that Galavetz is making her pitch before the ethics officers, because promoting that generalized aura of goodwill is an integral part of the "One Company, One Team" mission of the ethics program. Indeed, when people at Lockheed Martin talk about diversity, they are most likely referring in the first instance to the variety of products, ways of doing business, and cultures of the many "heritage companies" that make up the corporation. The differences between African Americans and Latinos seem trivial when weighed in corporate terms against the difference between a former division of IBM in Pennsylvania that makes systems software and a former plant of General Dynamics in

Texas that manufactures F-16 fighter jets. Each of the units that have been swallowed up by the new Lockheed Martin has its own practices, culture, and history, sometimes stretching back half a century or more. Creating "synergy" among these diverse units is one of the most pressing concerns of senior management.

The code of conduct, the annual ethics awareness program, a corporation-wide 800 "ethics help line"—these are intended to reach every single member of the Lockheed Martin corporation. They represent an attempt to recreate the sense of "family" for which the Lockheed part of its heritage was known, back when its operations were based principally in California. The omnipresence of the six company "values" constitutes a genuine commitment to promoting the idea of good business practice, a genuine fear of public exposure and federal investigations, and a genuine expectation that a more unified corporation will be a more profitable corporation.

The Orlando conference is a celebration of the accomplishments of the ethics operation, and a four-day pep talk for the ethics officers. The corporation's investment in ethics is substantial, and the operation's success in winning a majority of the corporation's employees over to its theme is tangible. Yet underlying the upbeat rhetoric of "mission success" and "one company, one team," there is a nagging sense of doubt. If ethics is so important to the company's mission, why does the career path of an ethics officer seem so marginal in the corporation structure? If the corporation's values are implanted so firmly, why does the prospect of the "bad apple" strike so much fear? Ethics seems easy when times are good, and when the corporation is showing its public face. But what happens under the pressures of the deadline, of the bottom line?

Like "diversity," "ethics" at Lockheed Martin means something broad, blandly acceptable, unarguable. Yet the very breadth of the definition (anything that an employee thinks is an ethics problem *is* an ethics problem) conceals the strict boundaries that the corporation erects around the field. Diversity in the Lockheed Martin context embraces words like "tolerance" and "respect," but avoids difficult engagements with race, ethnicity, and other sensitive areas of human difference. Ethics in the Lockheed Martin context embraces generalized concepts like honesty and integrity, but evades difficult engagements with issues that go to the very core of the corporation's business and mission. The boundaries in Lockheed Martin's ethics program create its coherence, its strength, and its esprit de corps. But the boundaries also threaten the corporation's credibility—first to the outside world, and eventually, perhaps to its own employee community.

Before exploring the vulnerabilities, however, it is important to recognize how much Lockheed Martin's current ethics and business program has already accomplished. At least five major factors plant that program on a firm foundation:

- **Breadth.** Lockheed Martin's program reaches every corner of the corporation, actively engaging employees at every level, and creating a strong consciousness about at least the rhetorical importance of ethics and values. The sustained commitment of time, personnel, money, and other resources to the program is genuine and impressive.
- **Creativity.** The corporation discovered early on that ethics needed not just to be discussed, but to be "marketed" if it was going to have a genuine impact. The ethics program has succeeded in arousing interest in, even passion about, issues of values, by creating formats that *engage* employees, rather than simply "teaching" them. The gamelike format of the awareness program, combined with innovations like the film festival, has helped to create an atmosphere where ethics is debated, not simply tolerated.
- **Values, not just compliance.** Lockheed Martin has been a leader in understanding that its programs need to do more than just tell people how to follow the rules. Following the rules *is* important, especially in an industry where the rules are so complex and often contradictory. But key principles of Lockheed Martin's program are that the rules do not cover every imaginable situation, that individuals need to be empowered to make good decisions, and that an internalization of values is one important factor in good decision making.
- **Strong endorsement from leadership.** The direct involvement of the senior leadership of the corporation has been crucial to the development of Lockheed Martin's program. Norm Augustine's stint in the first *Dilbert* video is legendary throughout the cor-

porate ethics world, and the continuing support for the ethics program through changes in leadership since 1995 has enabled the program to thrive.

- **Continuous evaluation and improvement.** The ethics office's employee surveys are at the forefront of a steady process of internal examination of the strengths and weaknesses of the corporation's ethics program. The capacity to build on strengths and face shortcomings honestly gives the program a suppleness that has served it well in the past, and is the best protection against staleness and complacency in the future. Through sharing with the DII, publishing the results of internal evaluations, and even allowing a researcher access to materials and programs, Lockheed Martin has also shown an admirable commitment to making its ethics program visible and open to criticism—another crucial element in allowing for continuous improvement.

Lockheed Martin has applied its "can-do," engineering culture to developing its ethics program. A problem was identified. A team of people was created to tackle the problem. The team experimented with various methods, working within a specific set of parameters: The program had to reach everyone in the corporation, it had to be clear and comprehensible, and it had to be measurable. With those parameters in mind, the corporation created from scratch a new and dynamic unit, and empowered that organization through committing money, time, and the public backing of senior management. Surveys, online databases, and ethics officer records document hundreds of thousands of ethics interactions each year. The ethics program may not break any flight speed records, nor will its firepower threaten the enemies of liberty, but it nevertheless represents a triumph of an engineering culture: a clean, elegant structure to contain the inherent messiness of nature and the human experience.

The ethics officers do not pretend that they have created an airtight system. Indeed, the Lockheed Martin ethics officers see every scandal in their industry as a cautionary tale, and they recognize that a single renegade employee could bring down the whole careful structure that they have built. The corporation is not a family, or even a village, but a farflung metropolis, and the ethics officers expect to find, among the majority of good-hearted citizens, a tiny minority of workers who flout the company's ethics standards. But they believe that these individuals can be contained and identified if the message on values and ethics echoes loudly and persistently enough throughout the corporation.

Furthermore, the Lockheed Martin ethics leadership has understood that the message cannot echo loudly and persistently unless it is not only important but interesting. Beginning with *Dilbert* and the "Ethics Challenge" board game, the corporation has sought to build confidence in the program through strategic entertainment. The more recent ethics film festival has continued this spirit. The company's internal surveys, and my own observations, suggest that the corporation has had widespread success in sustaining interest and confidence—broadly, if not universally.

For its pains, Lockheed Martin has been widely hailed within the greater "ethics community" for its programs. Its activities meet and often exceed the experts' benchmarks. How-to books on business ethics cite the corporation's programs frequently, and Lockheed Martin has been honored with industry awards. In 2004, for example, a magazine called *Workforce Management* named Lockheed Martin the winner of its *Optimas* award for ethics, citing the company's commitment to the idea that "Good ethics is good business."[9] Since 1995, Lockheed Martin has been widely hailed as a leader this area, responding to historical challenges vigorously and effectively to develop a program that represents American business ethics at its best. As I have noted before, few other American institutions—in either the for-profit or the nonprofit world—have made so concerted and sustained an effort.

chapter four

Vulnerabilities

For all its successes, there are significant limitations to Lockheed Martin's approach to ethics. Measured against its own standards and those of the contemporary ethics industry, Lockheed Martin's program shines. Measured against the expectations of the broader culture, however, the program falls short.

There is a significant gap between how corporate America judges itself and how its ideas about values and integrity play out in the larger culture. Lockheed Martin's ethics program, for all its excellent qualities, illustrates that gap. One consequence of this gap is that the corporation's quest to be seen as an active force for good in American life remains, at best, incomplete. Another consequence is that the company's program is better at responding to the problems of the past than to the problems of the future.

Lockheed Martin's ethics program addresses people, but it does not address systems. The exclusive emphasis on lived individual experience is appealing and in many ways effective. But the impact of a corporation like Lockheed Martin is not simply the accretion of millions of acts of fundamental decency undertaken by 130,000 workers. It is also the impact of the corporation as a very powerful organization, or, rather, as a collection of very powerful organizations. Lockheed Martin's program is innovative in reaching the 130,000 employees, but that is not enough. Innovation for innovation, evil will eventually outflank virtue. It thrives not in the isolated human heart, but in the very spirit of collective enterprise that corporations value.

The gaps in the program are most apparent when it is examined in the light of the long-standing expectations in American life regarding corporate behavior. When it comes to addressing the moral character of the corporation's leaders, the conduct of the corporation toward its customers and competitors, the company's treatment of its employees, its impact on its various communities, and the ethical considerations regarding profit within its industry, Lockheed Martin's programs leave major questions untouched. By drawing strict boundaries around their ethics enterprises, American corporations risk losing the public credibility that they are working so hard to maintain.

One way to look at this is to ask of Lockheed Martin's program a series of simple questions that grow out of the historical conceptions of business ethics that I discussed in chapter 1:

- Does the program specifically and effectively address the dangers of unethical leadership, of possible misbehavior among the corporation's most senior executives?
- Does the program take into account the dangers of *organizational* behavior, as well as individual misdeeds?
- Does the program convincingly address the needs and concerns of rank-and-file employees of the corporation?
- Does the program convincingly tackle the full range of issues involved in assessing the corporation's ultimate impact on its local, regional, national, and global communities?

The answers to these questions suggest that Lockheed Martin's program fails to go as far as it could, creating potential areas of vulnerability for the future.

1. Leadership: sidestepping privilege and power. The ethics program makes little special effort to target and address ethics issues involving the men and women at the very pinnacle of the corporate hierarchy. Although the program enjoys considerable support from top management, and senior executives participate in the basic ethics awareness activities, there is little evidence to suggest that the program offers enough attention to the specific challenges facing those who have the power and authority to err on the grandest scale.

2. Personal responsibility, collective innocence. Lockheed Martin's program lavishes attention on the individual employee, encouraging a strong sense of personal investment in the corporation's ethical performance. But the program does not take into account the pernicious side of organizational life: the tendency of groups to slide, often unintentionally, into habits of misconduct.

3. The corporate family: rewards and resistance. The ethics office has taken great pains to reach out to the corporation's employee base and make the organization supportive, rather than didactic. Nevertheless, there is always a fine line between social improvement and social control.

4. Policy and mission: ethics and judgment. Lockheed Martin's ethics program focuses on issues of business conduct, with few formal mechanisms for assessing the ethical implications of larger policy or strategic decisions of the corporation. The separation between "administrative ethics" and "policy ethics," quite common in American corporate life, leaves a gaping hole that can undermine the credibility of the ethics program and its ultimate effectiveness.

For all its successes, these important gaps in Lockheed Martin's program may leave the corporation vulnerable to new forms of scandal, and new sources of public outrage. In describing these gaps, I do not mean to suggest that the company's *performance* in these areas is necessarily deficient. I am saying, instead, that I am not convinced that the ethics program as currently conceived is well positioned to *prevent* problems in these areas that might arise in the future. To the extent that a good ethics program is supposed to be preventive rather than reactive, these strike me as significant shortcomings. In each section, I include recommendations for how the problems might be conceived or addressed in the future. I realize that I am not aware of all the possible internal constraints that might prevent such recommendations from being implemented, but if I am going to criticize, I feel a responsibility to offer starting points for remedies that might serve as the basis for future reflection, debate, and possibly change.

Leadership: Sidestepping Privilege and Power

Many of the most spectacular corporate scandals in the first years of the twenty-first century have had their origins in the plushest executive suites. At Adelphia and Tyco, the leaders of the corporations were charged with naked plunder of the assets of the organization. At Enron and WorldCom, senior executives appear to have gone to extraordinary lengths to deceive government regulators and the public, not to mention their own employees, about the true financial circumstances of the corporations. At Boeing, senior executives acted as though they believed that ordinary rules of conflict of interest did not apply at the very highest levels of industry and government. In each of these cases, and in many others, the direct or indirect responsibility for the misdeeds landed eventually at the doorstep of the chief executive officer (CEO) himself. Not every scandal originates with corporate leadership, but when megacorporations grow as large and powerful as those in the United States today, it is obvious that those with the most power usually have the capacity to do the greatest damage. Every once in a while, the scurrilous actions of a minor player will bring down a major international institution, as happened with Baring's Bank. But it is far more likely that a corporate scandal that makes the front page of the *New York Times* will involve senior executives with direct responsibility for millions of dollars worth of assets and business. There are at least three factors that can push senior executives to testing the boundaries of ethics and integrity: opportunity, incentive, and the very self-confidence that makes them successful in the first place.

By the nature of their positions, senior executives in any organization have more opportunity to act badly on a grand scale. Senior executives have more power, more access, more influence, and often less accountability than more junior members of the organization. They control resources, they control information, and they make more decisions involving more people and more money. Fewer people oversee their work, and those who have the best access to the inner workings of their decisions are often powerless to advise or influence those actions. Opportunity does not in and of itself create temptation or erode character. There is no reason to think that corporate leaders, by virtue of their position, are any less "moral" than others in their organization or the larger society. But malicious or ill-considered decisions made at the top of the corporate hierarchy will by definition be more consequential than those made further down the line.

Men and women at the top often also have greater incentive to cross an ethical boundary. Sometimes this is a matter of pure greed and large numbers. The members of the Rigas family looked at Adelphia's assets and saw the chance to siphon tens of millions of dollars from the company's assets into their personal accounts. With the size and power of modern corporations, senior executives can sometimes find themselves tempted by almost unimaginable financial rewards if they are willing to bend the rules. Incentive, however, is not just a matter of naked greed. The vagaries of the market in a world of rapidly fluctuating profits and losses create enormous pressures on senior executives to succeed, or at least not to fail. These negative incentives place a premium on creating at least the appearance of a positive financial outlook, especially to the investment community. Corporate leaders, whose careers rise and fall on the basis of earnings, assets, and stock performance, have the greatest incentive to rewrite the rules to place their own work in the best possible light.

In addition to falling prey to opportunity and incentive, senior executives can be undone by their own strength of character. Independence, creativity, defying conventional thinking, risk taking—these are qualities essential to strong leadership, and they are often justly rewarded within an organizational hierarchy, as dynamic leadership over the past half century at Lockheed and Lockheed Martin has shown. They are also qualities that can make an individual vulnerable to making choices to suit his or her own needs and preferences. Again, this is not to argue that those who defy conventional thinking about business strategy are destined to defy conventional thinking about ethics. But it seems obvious that some significant proportion of those succeed through brash new thinking will eventually come to believe that their own actions are not only inherently profitable but inherently "right." There will always be a fine line between self-confidence and hubris.

Lockheed Martin's own history suggests its vulnerability to renegade behavior at the top. The global bribery scandals of the 1960s and 1970s involved a number of individuals at the upper echelons of Lockheed, men whose work and contacts made it easy to develop special relationships and make special payments that lubricated the corporation's overseas business. Lockheed's deepening financial crisis in the early 1970s put enormous pressure on senior management. When corporation president Carl Kotchian launched his personal campaign to sell the TriStar jet in Japan, he was taking on himself the burden of avoiding a darker financial abyss. Kotchian's strategy of secret negotiations and payments owed something to his confidence in his own commitments, in his conviction that the good of the corporation was a greater moral good than certain niceties of business conduct.

History also suggests another challenge for corporate leaders: Those at the top face the most complex ethical dilemmas, and encounter situations that are most susceptible to changing moral standards. The nineteenth-century titans of industry thought of themselves, by and large, as men of character who put their own stamp of values on the companies they built. By their own lights, and by the standards of their youth, they operated according to clear sets of principles. But the very success of their enterprises created new realities and new environments in the United States—a landscape crisscrossed with railroads, vertically integrated corporations, and efficient communications networks—that created whole new generations of ethics issues. What the titans believed was creative exploitation of opportunity appeared to their competitors and to succeeding generations to be crass exploitation of people and resources. In hindsight, we recognize that the corporate leaders of the era were able to think of themselves as beacons of morality because it took years for the public and the government to define and react to new fangled abuses like pools, trusts, deceptive advertising, and the exploitation of workers. In some ways, this pattern continued through the twentieth century and encompassed the more recent scandals involving Lockheed and other defense contractors. The globalization of American business during the 1950s meant that bribery overseas became a way of life, tolerated as morally acceptable in a world of relative standards. Under the glare of the Washington spotlight, Carl Kotchian portrayed himself as an American patriot and a company loyalist who was the victim of a hypocritical political vendetta.

In the contemporary environment, the ground is shifting even more rapidly under today's senior executives, and the ethics issues at the top of the hierarchy are increasingly complex. If a low-level employee knowingly mischarges labor to the wrong account, or neglects safety checks, or inadvertently shares proprietary information and then tries to cover his or her tracks, these are straightforward situations that require straightforward investigations and response. The senior executives at Lockheed Martin, however, operate in an environment where their daily decisions have enormous impact, not only on the corporation itself but also on the outside world. They operate in a world of relationships and deals and negotiations where the rules are often not clear-cut, where innovation and success require unconventional approaches, where new arrangements are shifting the ethical ground. The complex arrangements involved in major mergers and acquisitions, for example, create an enormous array of ethical minefields. The instigation of complex accounting practices that might have an impact on investors, the potential disruption for employees, assessing the ethical climate of a takeover target, the protection and the sharing of proprietary information—these types of issues create special challenges for senior executives in situations where a mistake can be enormously costly not only to a career, but to the corporation and even the country. Equally complicated is the web of relationships between senior executives at Lockheed Martin, their peers in the defense industry, and their counterparts in the U.S. government. The maze of competition and collaborations creates ample opportunities for personal and professional favors to trump forthright business practice.

With these factors in mind, it would make sense to expect that a corporate ethics program would place special emphasis on issues of power and leadership, and that it would put special safeguards in place to address the particular challenges facing those in leadership positions. However broad-based a corporation's program may be, it makes more sense to judge its merits by its attention to problems at the top of the hierarchy, rather than at the bottom.

Lockheed Martin makes three important claims about its ethics program in regard to senior leadership. First, the corporation touts the solid and highly visible support of its ethics program by the CEO and other members of the leadership team. Second, the corporation makes it clear that all members of its senior management team not only participate fully in the annual ethics training, but also complete dozens of other modules each year that are designed for others within their areas of responsibility. Third, the corporation makes clear that the ethics officers are widely available for consultation with members of senior management. Each of these elements of Lockheed Martin's ethics program is worthy and important, but they nevertheless fall short of addressing the ethical demands of leadership in all their complexity.

Where Lockheed's corporate leadership was an ethical liability in the 1970s, one of the company's great successes of the past decade has been to reverse this process, so that the identification of the corporation's leadership with the ethics program is now a strength. CEO Norm Augustine staked his own reputation on the ability of the company to produce a high-quality, high-impact ethics program, and he was willing to take chances in the face of considerable skepticism in order to pull it off. Augustine and his successors, Vance Coffman and Robert Stevens, clearly deserve credit for the strides that the corporation has taken in this area since 1995.

Personal integrity and strong support for an ethics program are not, however, the same thing as having a *system* that aims to ensure continuous integrity at the top of the corporate hierarchy. Support from the leadership may be necessary to launch a successful ethics program, but that support provides no guarantee that those same leaders will necessarily act for the best in their capacity as corporate decisionmakers. After all, it is perfectly conceivable for an individual to offer the strongest possible public support for an ethics program, while violating ethical standards as a matter of habit in his or her day-to-day work. This is known as hypocrisy, of course, but any strong ethics program should be prepared for that possibility. A more common scenario, perhaps, involves the subtle but steady erosion of values under the stress of the workplace. A corporate leader may enter a position with a strong set of values and convictions, only to find them chipped away by circumstances. It casts no aspersions on the personal character and commitment of Norm Augustine or Vance Coffman or any other Lockheed Martin leader to suggest that their public commitment to the ethics program is no more than a necessary starting point. For the program that they have spawned to be ultimately effective, it will need to train its sights on the behavior of the CEO and other senior executives, skeptically discounting their pronouncements and focusing more closely on their actions.

It is a fine thing, symbolically, to emphasize that senior executives at Lockheed Martin undergo the same kinds of trainings and modules as thousands of other employees of the corporation. If leadership, however, requires special skills and makes special ethical demands, does it not require an ethics curriculum more suited to its level of complexity? As we have seen, the corporation's ethics awareness program and training modules do an excellent job of provoking discussion among a wide range of employees, but they tackle ethics issues at a relatively low level of complexity. None of these many trainings, as far as I can tell, addresses the special ethical demands placed on those at the highest reaches of the hierarchy. Ethics, after all, is ultimately about the just application of power. Just as we know that the business situations that senior executives face are inherently more complex and challenging, so are the questions about the proper application of values in any particular situation. The ethics and compliance modules favored at Lockheed Martin make the law clear, suggest sources of help, and hint that many situations have no single "right answer," but they do little to encourage the deep, difficult self-examination that can help leaders stave off opportunity, incentive, and their own hubris. The program encourages employees to think about the complexities of applying the rules and regulations, but it does little to encourage those at the top to think about the complex nature of the rules themselves. Sheer quantity of exposure to ethics modules cannot replace more searching considerations of the ethical challenges of power and leadership. The 2003 scandals at Boeing illustrate vividly that an extensive, broad-based ethics program creates insufficient protections against top executives who believe that they can redefine ethical boundaries with impunity.

The ethics officers at Lockheed Martin are available for consultation with the leaders of their divisions, but the effectiveness and extent of this consultation depend on personal relationships, rather than on more formal practice. Alice Edmonds at the Lockheed Martin Space Operations division in Virginia described to me at length the ways that her company president relies on her advice in key situations. And CEO Bob Stevens is known to drop in for advice at the office of ethics vice-president Maryanne Lavan. My impression is that these relationships are sometimes substantial, and that ethics officers have worked their way into positions of greater trust and responsibility vis-à-vis senior executives in recent years. But it is a relationship that is wholly at the discretion of the senior executive himself or herself, so it offers a relatively weak wall of protection against misdeeds at the top.

So, while Lockheed Martin's senior executives have offered considerable support to the ethics program over the past ten years, the program makes relatively modest demands on them, and opens up an area of vulnerability for the future. This is exacerbated by potential weaknesses in the structure of accountability. Ultimate authority on ethics issues at Lockheed Martin lies with the Audit and Ethics (A&E) Committee of the corporation's board of directors. The vice-president for ethics and business conduct reports to this committee, as well as to the CEO, so one strength of the structure is that there is a formal and direct line of communication between the ethics program and the board. The A&E committee does receive reports about higher level legal and ethics violations, and theoretically, at least this committee would be open to hearing concerns from the ethics office about the behavior of senior management. The 2002 Sarbanes-Oxley Act put significant pressure on corporate boards to play a more active role in overseeing ethics in their organizations, including the threat of holding directors personally liable for scandals that occur on their watch. So the board does have significant incentive to pay close attention to ethics and compliance issues.

As with so many corporations, however, the composition of Lockheed Martin's board does little to reassure outsiders that it can serve as a truly independent watchdog of corporate activities. Of fourteen members of the corporation's Board in 2004–2005, four were current or former senior executives at Lockheed Martin, two were senior executives at other major defense contractors, and one was recently retired from the U.S. Air Force. Most have served as directors of other major U.S. corporations, including Enron and Global Crossing. None of the Lockheed Martin executives sat on the six-member Audit and Ethics Committee, but its members were nevertheless part of an interlocking web of industry and government relationships. E. C. "Pete" Aldridge, a member of the Audit and Ethics Committee, is a former Undersecretary of Defense as well as a former senior executive at McDonnell-Douglas and the CEO of the Aerospace Corporation. Aldridge was a member of Lockheed Martin's board of directors, while at the same time heading a presidential commission that called in spring 2004 for privatizing much of NASA. Aldridge told the *New York Times* that he saw no conflict of interest, despite the fact that a division of Lockheed Martin, United Space Alliance, was a potential beneficiary of privatization.[1] Even where board members are individually men and women of impeccable reputations, the mirror-image profiles of so many directors make it difficult to believe fully in the thoroughness of their oversight, even with looming presence of Sarbanes-Oxley and the federal sentencing guidelines.

The question, then, is whether Lockheed Martin's ethics program is best positioned to protect the corporation against misdeeds by its top executives, and whether it can identify and stay ahead of emerging ethics issues that involve the top leadership. Lockheed Martin ethics officers fret that a "bad apple" like Michael Sears at Boeing can undo years of work, but there is a fatalism in the "bad apple" theory that dodges the issue. The Lockheed Martin *does* educate senior management about the specific type of violation in the Boeing case. Indeed, when the news broke in December 2003, Vance Coffman ordered that all relevant Lockheed Martin employees make sure that they were up-to-date on the compliance module on offering employment to U.S. government officials. But when it comes to more subtle forms of arm twisting, influence peddling, and relationship building, the program is silent. This is a matter both of education (providing senior executives with the opportunity to examine ethics issues in a manner suitable to their level of authority) and of accountability (creating credible mechanisms for monitoring the actions of senior executives).

It is also a matter of viewing ethics broadly enough to respond to changing public perceptions of what is right and what is wrong in corporate life. As recently as a decade ago, the salaries of a corporation's top executives were thought of simply as an internal management issue. But in an era when the gap between the richest and poorest workers in the United States has widened considerably, executive compensation has become an emerging ethics issue in the American corporate landscape. In 2003, Vance Coffman's total compensation package was more than $20,000,000, in a year when the total shareholder return for Lockheed Martin was down by 10 percent. In a newly skeptical era, this raises significant questions. Is it "right" for the CEO of a corporation to earn, for example, more than 200 times the salary of one of the corporation's ethics officers? Is it "right" for senior executives to earn large salaries, and sometimes larger bonuses, at a time when the owners of the corporation, its shareholders, are losing money? When does executive compensation cross the line and become simply too much? In other words, when does a compensation issue become an ethics issue?[2]

For Lockheed Martin's ethics officers, this issue is entirely off the table. Not a problem in our environment, Brian Sears assures me. "With all the oversight that we're getting from the federal government, there's no way that we're going to get away with anything excessive," Sears says. Besides, he goes on, "You couldn't pay me enough to do Dr. Coffman's job—to have to answer to so many constituencies, to work under so much pressure. He's worth every penny that they pay him."

Brian Sears may well be right—perhaps the Lockheed Martin CEO's compensation would stand up to every test of fairness known to humankind. The point, however, is not to make a judgment about what Vance Coffman or Bob Stevens earns. The point is that the issue is not *registered* in terms of fairness or ethics in the Lockheed Martin environment. Without that type of scrutiny, the corporation is vulnerable to the kinds of cozy compensation deals at other companies that have spawned notorious headlines in recent years. Even if the deals are not excessive in contemporary terms, a bland disregard for the income gap may be seen as morally blind by a future generation. It is possible that the issue of executive compensation receives rigorous scrutiny in ethical terms among the corporation's leadership and board of directors. But even if this is true, the public silence on the issue undermines the corporation's self-image as an organization willing to tackle the full range of tough questions.

Taken together, these concerns suggest that Lockheed Martin's program has not fully addressed the ethical challenges of corporate leadership. Of course, there are limits. At a certain point, any ethics program has to depend on trust, goodwill, and the efficacy of its initial efforts. No organization can station an independent ethics officer behind every executive's desk chair, and none wants to "train" its executives to the point of numbness. But there are, perhaps, four types of steps that a corporation like Lockheed Martin could take to address both the substance and the appearance of effective ethics programs for its top management.

1. It could develop ethics programs that address the specific problems and the specific level of complexity of the work of senior executives. Lockheed Martin took a small step in this direction by developing "Ethics Tools for Leaders," a program for all 15,000 managers throughout the corporation. But this program is really aimed at mid-level supervisors and focuses on issues of managing people, rather than issues of more generalized power and authority. Perhaps senior executives could spend less time on compliance modules, and more time examining cases that pertain directly to decision making at their own level and that encourage them to look back with a critical eye on decisions that they have already taken, with an eye toward lessons for the future.

2. The corporation could create a stronger and more formal role for the ethics office in advising and monitoring the actions of top executives. Informal consultation is helpful, but it is most helpful to those who are already inclined to think most carefully about potential ethics problems. A more formal structure for this type of consultation would create one additional opportunity to head off problems before they occur.

3. The corporation could appoint members to the board of directors with specific professional expertise in corporate ethics. Such appointments would strengthen at least the appearance, and perhaps the substance, of independent oversight by the Audit and Ethics Committee.

4. Lockheed Martin could be more courageous and transparent about framing and publicly tackling emerging ethics issues, such as executive compensation. The company's policies in this area (and other emerging areas) may be fully defensible in ethical terms, but this can only be borne out through open discussion of the issues involved. Such openness, incidentally, could have positive effects on morale within the company, as well as bolstering confidence in the larger community about the corporation's willingness to take on difficult questions.

Experts in the field always insist that a strong corporate ethics program has to start with character and support at the top. In the past ten years, Lockheed Martin has been blessed with exactly this kind of visible leadership, and those leaders have helped to create a strong and vibrant program. The irony is that despite this public commitment, ethics-minded corporate leaders like those at Lockheed Martin may ultimately be judged by history as harshly as the nineteenth-century titans of industry—and for the same reasons. They put every issue to an ethical test—except for the special powers and privileges of their own position.

Personal Responsibility, Collective Innocence

As we have seen, Lockheed Martin's ethics program places a premium on informing and empowering the individual decisionmaker. The program is "driven down" to every corner of the corporation, and the code of ethics and the training modules encourage every employee to shoulder his or her share of the responsibility for maintaining the corporation's values. This approach democratically distributes a sense of individual investment in the company's ethical well-being, and it has helped improve the company's performance on business conduct issues. But it also means that the program bypasses a crucial dimension of organizational ethics: the dynamics of collective decision making.

It is instructive, in this context, to examine the continuing ethics and compliance problems that Lockheed Martin has faced over the past decade. We have already seen that Lockheed Martin is candid about the fact that its programs will never be fully able to eradicate misconduct. The corporation has managed to avoid major scandal since the 1995 merger, but it has still been involved in dozens of cases involving allegations of legal and ethical wrongdoing. In 2003, the Project on Government Oversight (POGO) found that Lockheed Martin (and its heritage companies) had been involved in eighty-four instances of alleged misconduct and settlements for the period since 1990, with fines and settlements totaling at least $426,000,000 during that period.[3] The corporation was second only to General Electric (eighty-seven instances during the same period). These numbers, by themselves, say little about the effectiveness of the corporation's ethics program. The POGO database lumps together settlements, pending cases, and allegations, so the totals by themselves are somewhat misleading. But they provide a rough indication of the continuing challenge that the corporation's ethics and compliance program faces.

More important than the totals is the nature of the violations, especially those that reached a final settlement. The list of Lockheed Martin's violations spans the country and the corporation's many enterprises:

- In 1996, the corporation settled a civil lawsuit for $67,000,000 in a case involving environmental contamination in Burbank, California, after it closed its original headquarters; the company has also been forced to settle a number of other cases involving environmental contamination in such locales as Colorado, Vermont, and other California locations.
- NASA won $7,100,000 in a 2003 lawsuit claiming that Lockheed Martin Engineering Sciences Corporation charged the space agency for false and fraudulent lease cost claims.
- A judgment against Lockheed Martin Electromechanical Systems in 2000 generated a $500,000 fine and $7,500,000 in restitution for a case where the company charged the U.S. Navy for costs incurred on its private commercial contracts.

- Lockheed Martin incurred a $13,000,000 fine in 2000 for providing information to the Chinese government that could potentially be used for developing missiles.
- The corporation's Naval Electronics & Surveillance Systems company settled a suit for $4,500,000 in 2000 involving improper use of Foreign Military Sales funds.
- In 2002, twenty-six recently terminated employees of the corporation's Knolls Atomic Power Laboratory won a judgment of nearly $6,000,000 when they filed suit for age discrimination.
- A 2003 settlement of more than $37,000,000 addressed cost overruns on four contracts for the purchase of navigation and targeting pods with the U.S. Air Force.[4]

The POGO database covers only the most public types of legal and ethical violations. Lockheed Martin's own ethics database tracks a much more extensive set of investigations and settlements, involving not only corporate misbehavior but also the deportment of individual employees. The corporation chooses not to share this data, but the ethics officers assert that their internal statistics show a marked decline in significant cases over the past eight years. Nevertheless, they are still tracking hundreds of cases each year, with dozens involving significant violations of the company's code.

Lockheed Martin's explanation for the range and scope of these settlements comes down to one word: size. Yes, ethics officers say, misconduct unhappily does occur. It is impossible to rid the organization entirely of bad apples, when the organization involves 130,000 people and more than $25 billion in business each year. Besides, some of these violations took place in companies that had been recently acquired by Lockheed Martin; this means that in some cases the offenses occurred before the company was part of the Lockheed Martin "family," and in other cases that the corporation's values had not yet had time to take hold when the violations occurred. Ethics officers also point out that some of the more dramatic cases were brought by whistleblowers who stood to profit personally by identifying problems within the corporation; in the 2003 mischarging case, for example, a former Lockheed Martin employee was awarded $8.7 million as part of the settlement.

It is reasonable to suppose that Lockheed Martin's ethics program has helped to head off ethics disasters and to reduce the corporation's over-all exposure to incidences of fraud and abuse. Yet the ongoing list of cases suggests that size may itself be a catalyst as well as an excuse. The sheer breadth of corporation activity means that a centralized values program can only penetrate so far, and that there are nearly boundless opportunities for chicanery—whether for personal benefit or in sup-port of the company's bottom line. The sheer size of the company is also, importantly, a protection against the harshest penalty for wrongdoing: loss of business. The evidence suggests that the U.S. military is so de-pendent on a small number of major defense contractors that it cannot afford to withhold too much business from Lockheed Martin and its largest competitors.[5]

Even within a gigantic enterprise, the ethics program makes it more difficult for an individual to perpetrate fraud or abuse either through in-tention or through ignorance. Lockheed Martin's program puts the onus on the individual to know the legal and ethical rules, and it alerts employees to illegal or illicit activities of their fellow employees. The program creates an atmosphere where it is, in theory, more difficult for an individual to get away with cutting ethical corners, even if the com-pany has not been as successful as it wants in encouraging employees to report unethical behavior that they have witnessed. The workshops and training modules ensure that ignorance on the part of an employee can-not be an excuse. The program also gives the corporation a measure of protection from formal responsibility for the actions of rogue workers.

However, the types of corporate malfeasance illustrated in Lockheed Martin's recent history are seldom the result of a single individual's ac-tions. Overcharging on a contract with the Navy involves more than a single person's manipulation of a spreadsheet. If too much information is made available to a foreign government in a particular set of business transactions, it involves the participation of many individuals who are making complex choices together as they try to meet goals and serve their customer. A pattern of age discrimination likely involves the hiring practices of dozens of managers, each of whom may be trying to do his or her job as effectively as possible, but who collectively may be perpe-trating an injustice.

In any organization, the most important decisions are seldom judg-ments made by individuals in their solitary capacity as "decision makers."

This is particularly true in an engineering culture, where teamwork, shared information, and cooperation among different groups are the lifeblood of the organization. People work together closely on projects, share ideas, push each other to find innovative solutions to problems, and make decisions together about how to bring the best ideas to fruition. This work style makes for a productive and exciting environment, but it also creates a particular challenge for living by company values, because people in groups are much more likely to push the boundaries of ethical behavior than individuals acting on their own. Several evasions of ethical responsibility tempt the individual working in a team. He can say to himself that if no one else has voiced an objection to a particular course of action, then it must be acceptable. She can convince herself that the general direction that a team is taking has been endorsed by the team leader or by a superior in the hierarchy. Or, most simply, an individual can decide that responsibility for weighing the ethical implications of a decision lies with some other member of the group. Important decisions do not simply happen at key moments, but they occur over time, often through an accretion of actions. Indeed, it is frequently impossible to pinpoint the precise moment that a course of action becomes a settled fact, and it is often equally impossible to identify clear responsibility when things go particularly right or particularly wrong. Ultimately, any strong, sustained ethics program needs consciously to address the elusive dynamic of collective decisionmaking, and to create mechanisms for addressing organizational culture, not just the values of individual actors.

The Lockheed Martin ethics program borrows the *form* of collective decision making, but the *content* is focused exclusively on the individual. In the ethics awareness program, employees talk in teams about situations facing individuals, but nothing in the program's content challenges them to take on the complex problems of collective responsibility. The program breaks ethics down into a series of discrete, small decisions, leaving the larger context of those decisions virtually untouched. The program is cognizant of the potential problem of wayward "groupthink," but it counts on the power of the courageous individual to stand up and challenge the collective wisdom that is pushing a decision across an ethical boundary. This approach demands a great deal from the individual actor, perhaps more than is realistic in many situations. More importantly, it assumes that key decision points are clear, crisp, identifiable moments when a right-minded intervention can prevent disaster. This may not always be the case.

Furthermore, the vast bulk of the resources of the ethics and business conduct division is concentrated on relatively minor problems. Ethics officers spend a great deal of their time on everyday situations involving issues like personnel problems, side businesses, and access to pornography via the corporation's computers. Cases in the ethics awareness program likewise present scenarios where the stakes are comparatively low. The by-product of a well-intentioned effort to make ethics issues accessible throughout the corporation is a lack of attention to big-picture, systemic forces that lead to major problems.

It is no secret that some of the worst abuses of human values in the last century have been committed by "decent" men and women who were simply trying to do their job. Working together, they find themselves seduced by the goals of their common enterprise: the company, the army, the nation. The greater good of the organization trumps local concerns: Some people are simply bound to get hurt in the competition for profit and survival. Lockheed Martin's program has responded actively to long-standing concerns about the business practices of American corporations, vastly reducing the ability of individual actors to perpetrate fraud and abuse. But the corporation's vast effort misses the mark when it comes to collective action, and this leaves Lockheed Martin vulnerable to modern-day equivalents of the "pools" and "trusts" that besmirched American industry a century ago. It could take steps to head off these problems in two ways:

1. The trainings and modules that the ethics program offers could address challenges of group dynamics more directly. The discussion-based approach to the ethics awareness program is a good start, but the atomization of most of the training modules, undertaken by individuals on their own computers or PDAs, stresses individual decision making. A more explicit awareness of collective decision making would help diminish reliance on the heroic individual.

2. The ethics and business conduct division could play a more direct role in helping units audit and assess vulnerabilities in their organizational culture, both by dissecting previous cases of collective wrongdoing and by making candid assessments of the current climate.[6]

The Corporate "Family": Rewards and Resistance

If we look at Lockheed Martin's ethics program through the lens of the labor environment, we see a highly self-conscious attempt to create a new kind of corporate culture. Ethics officers see their job as not only education and investigation, but also to provide a unifying theme for a far-flung enterprise, to create unity by creating virtue. This approach has had some noted successes, but it has also provoked resistance to a program that can sometimes be seen as condescending and controlling.

Because company policies lie, for the most part, outside the boundaries of the corporation's ethics program, it is not obvious what mechanisms will allow company values to protect workers in times of financial stress. The program pays a great deal of attention to the actions of individual managers with respect to individual employees. Cases in the training programs focus on issues of sexual harassment, or favoritism, or fairness in promotion procedures, with attention to the actions of both workers and their supervisors. Policies involving wage scales, benefits, disciplinary procedures, and hiring practices, however, are matters for the human resources department. No doubt many of the individuals in human resource departments at Lockheed Martin bring full and complex ideas about ethics into their discussions, but there is no sustained and consistent method for making ethics considerations a central feature of developing employment policies.

Instead of focusing on employment policies, the ethics program concentrates on molding the lives and minds of individual employees to encourage them to embody the Lockheed Martin values. There are modern echoes of Ford Motor Company's efforts, almost a century ago, to develop the Five Dollar Day and the Sociological Department because the demands of the modern assembly line meant that the company needed a more reliable workforce. Ford set about deliberately to create a corporate culture that would mold character, reward virtuous behavior, and, in effect, ostracize workers who refused to toe the line. Just as Ford's "ethics" program responded to an advance in industrial technology— the mechanization of production—so does Lockheed Martin's. Lockheed's challenge lies in the maintaining the integrity of a huge and dispersed workforce, in an environment where individuals are empowered by virtue of high-speed communications. Ford needed workers who would demonstrate their loyalty to the company by showing up on time; Lockheed Martin needs workers who will put the company's well-being before personal opportunity. The modern corporation cannot, of course, bring its program directly into the home lives of its employees, but it can use the communications means at its disposal to exhort workers as a regular part of their lives on the job.

This emphasis on organizational values, however, produces its own counterreaction, fueled both by resistance to conformity and by cynicism about the corporation's intent. Phil Tenney, who conducts the biennial ethics survey, notes a persistent strain of anger among a minority of the respondents, men and women who find the ethics program oppressive and too "politically correct." These comments tend to come from areas of the corporation with significant numbers of blue-collar employees, responding to a gap that they perceive between tidy company rhetoric and the more complex messiness of daily life in any working environment.

This counterreaction took a tragic turn in the summer of 2003 at Lockheed Martin's aircraft parts facility in Meridian, Mississippi. On July 8, a forty-eight-year-old assembly-line worker named Doug Williams attended his annual ethics training session. Williams, who was White, had a history of altercations involving African American coworkers, and he had been known to complain about the compulsory nature of the ethics program. Shortly after the training session began, Williams went outside to his pickup truck, returned to the training room with a semiautomatic rifle and a shotgun, and started shooting. Two men were fatally wounded there, and Williams then went onto the factory floor and killed three more employees, before finally turning his gun on himself. Doug Williams was obviously a seriously disturbed individual, whose troubled history had been unfolding for many years. Nevertheless, the fact that the ethics session proved a trigger for his tragic spree hints at a reservoir of resentment against the dissemination of a culture of values.

The case of Doug Williams illustrates the difficulties in trying to impose a system of values on an employee community. On the one hand, to be effective and just, organizational culture must to some extent be coercive when it comes to values. In the weeks before his shooting spree, for example, Williams had taunted Black coworkers by wearing an improvised protective head covering that resembled a Ku Klux Klan hood; his manager had quite properly challenged and disciplined Williams on that occasion. Williams had done nothing "legally" wrong, but his supervisor recognized that his actions represented a threat to company values, and that strong action was necessary. On the other hand, a sustained attempt to create a values-based culture is bound to flirt with a climate of social control, which in turn may provoke resentment and rebellion. From the workers' point of view, the ultimate test is whether the corporation applies the same standards to its core activities as it does to the behavior of individual employees.

A case in point is the question of the diversity of the Lockheed Martin workforce. In recent years, the corporation has begun a national push in this area. With an aging workforce, a decline in Americans studying engineering, and the changing demographics of the United States, the corporation has recognized that broadening its pool of potential hires is a business imperative, especially with military spending on the upswing, and the prospect of adding major new projects in the next decade. Yet one can hear senior Lockheed Martin employees discuss "diversity" in the corporate workforce without making any reference to race or gender, or even discussing the possibility that the corporation might have a responsibility toward underrepresented groups in its ranks. "Diversity" in the Lockheed Martin context is more likely to mean tolerating an engineer with long hair or an earring, rather than developing programs to bring more women into engineering positions or making the growing Latino population central to the corporation's recruiting plans for the future. Of course, there is nothing wrong with expanding the company's dress code or listening to a younger generation's music at a company party. But the corporation's ethical obligations to underrepresented populations are off the ethics program's radar screen. The program does, of course, address and discourage discrimination against current employees. But it is not positioned to implement the corporation's values when it comes to promoting diversity in a positive sense through hiring, mentoring, promoting, and retaining minority employees. I do not mean to make a judgment here about Lockheed Martin's *performance* in recruiting, retaining, and promoting minority employees. Lockheed Martin has been subject to lawsuits and federal government investigations regarding its treatment of African American employees, most recently following the Meridien shootings, but it is difficult to assess the merits of those charges across the corporation.[7] The more important point is that the corporation's ethics program shines a spotlight on one possible area of discrimination (racism or harassment in the workplace) while leaving the larger policy questions (hiring and promotion practices) virtually untouched.

The Meridien case represents an atypical extreme, in more than one way. Nevertheless, the incident provides Lockheed Martin with the opportunity to reconsider the relationship between its ethics program and its human resources policies. The corporation's program is highly sensitive already to certain forms of workplace issues, especially the relationship between individual employees and their supervisors. Explicit discussion of the ethical implications of decisions about large-scale workplace issues could strengthen the program's credibility both inside and outside the corporation.[8]

Policy and Mission: Ethics and Judgment

Lockheed Martin's ethics program focuses on the areas of organizational activity that fall under the rubric of "business conduct." The program developed and thrived in response to a series of specific problems and scandals, involving violations of standards of business practice like bribery and mischarging. At Lockheed Martin, the ethics program, extensive as it is, stops at the border of business conduct. As in most other major corporations, the ethics program addresses ethical issues within the walls of the corporation: the behavior of company employees in highly specific situations.

American conceptions of "ethics," as we have seen, go well beyond these areas of business conduct, encompassing the way that a corporation does business in a larger sense: how it treats its employees, its impact on the communities it serves, and the impact of its core business on its society and the world at large. As we have seen in our look at American history, the broader public expects corporate ethics to include and embrace a thorough look at a corporation's policies, strategic decisions, community activities, and even its mission. This seems especially relevant for a corporation of Lockheed Martin's size, importance, and character. With its large employee base and geographical scope, the corporation is bound to have an enormous impact both inside and outside of its walls. As a player in a quasi-public industry, its influence on policy has a disproportionate impact on both national and international events. And as a weapons manufacturer, in the business of making products that kill people, Lockheed Martin encounters, in its core mission, a set of moral and ethical concerns that companies in less controversial industries might not face.

With these factors in mind, the segregation of ethics from questions of policy, community impact, and mission raises critical questions about the nature and purpose of an ethics program. What is the point, after all, of trumpeting a corporate ethics program, if it is not willing to take on the toughest and largest questions about a corporation's impact on the world?

Some people believe that this is, in fact, entirely the wrong question. They argue that it is critically important that American corporations make a clear distinction between "administrative ethics" and "policy ethics." For Stuart Gilman, former president of the Ethics Resource Center, combining these approaches leads inevitably to a "muddle" that ultimately produces paralysis. To Gilman, corporations should focus their attention on "administrative ethics"—running their organizations with both clear and consistent business practice standards, accompanied by a clear and consistent set of company values that transcend mere compliance with regulations and the law. This approach allows corporations to communicate a consistent message, empowering employees to create an atmosphere where integrity and profits can flourish symbiotically.

Gilman argues that if corporations formally incorporate the ethical dimensions of policy and mission into their ethics programs, they enter an open-ended domain that will ultimately endanger the whole project. He acknowledges that a company like Lockheed Martin faces a whole host of macro-level moral issues: "Let's face it, if you're making bombs, there is an ethics question about how they're going to be used." But he contends that virtually every industry faces a complex series of questions about the nature of its core business that simply cannot be tackled at an organizational level. Automobile manufacturers create products that make possible innumerable benefits for modern life, but they befoul the air and they cost tens of thousands of people their lives each year. Potato-chip manufacturers create products that taste good but make people fat and bring on heart disease. Defense contractors help protect the American way of life, but their products can lead to a destabilized world. Corporations simply do not have the capacity to address these issues internally—these belong to a larger social, political, and philosophical debate. Companies are better served by focusing on what they can do: run a clean organization based on strong values, and trust that the implementation of those values will encourage the organization to play a productive part in the world.

It would appear that Lockheed Martin follows this line of thinking. Its ethics program, as we have seen, concentrates on internal business practice matters. The ethics program is entirely separate from the division that most conspicuously focuses on the corporation's impact on the external world: the "community relations" program. Under this rubric, Lockheed Martin sponsors a host of national and local programs. Its most extensive programming in this area focuses on K–12 education, especially, true to the corporation's mission, in the sciences. It offers fellowships for math and science teachers in California, supports a teacher leadership center in Florida, and promotes interactive learning techniques in Texas. Lockheed Martin employees and retirees participate in the Network of Volunteer Associates (NOVA), tutor children in math and reading in Dallas, and have developed an online volunteer placement system in Owego, New York. The corporation supports music and dance companies in the state of Washington, and sponsors exhibitions and performances at such institutions as the National Museum of Women in the Arts, the Baltimore Museum of Art, and the John F. Kennedy Center in Washington, D.C.

These are worthy programs, and they represent a type of effort that makes an important contribution to American life. These activities also have important public relations value for the corporation, and as such, they represent a business strategy. The trend toward creating and marketing a corporate "soul" remains undiminished since the era documented by Roland Marchand. Indeed, if anything, the trend has increased, as pressure from the government, from public interest groups, and from consumers has persuaded companies to redouble their social outreach efforts to counteract negative publicity regarding their core activities. There is nothing inherently wrong with mixed motives. If a corporation's outreach programs benefit the company as well as the community, then both can win. Both can win, that is, as long as the big picture, the overall impact of the corporation's impact on its communities, remains in view.

A strict separation between "ethics" and "community relations" illustrates the problem with separating "administrative ethics" and "policy ethics." A corporation may give generously and create vibrant, positive community programs with one hand, while the other hand institutes policies and products that breed death and destruction. When Philip Morris aggressively advertises its community contributions, the company breeds cynicism, because its efforts are so obvious an attempt to distract the public from the lethal nature of its core products. When an industrial polluter helps support after-school youth programs, those activities ring hollow in light of the adverse effect of the toxins on children's health. These examples may represent the obvious end of the spectrum, but the principle holds just as true for organizations with less drastic public relations problems. Being a good corporate citizen is the whole package, not simply an accounting of dollars spent in schools and clinics.

By strictly separating ethics from corporate social responsibility, Lockheed Martin and other corporations evade a searching consideration of the big picture. The impact of the corporation's core business on the local economy, on government, on the environment, and on its neighbors remains unscrutinized in a formal way. But the bifurcation opens up a gaping hole that has the unfortunate effect of making both ethics and corporate social responsibility (CSR) look like window dressing. The ethics program appears to have an artificial border that protects the corporation from opening up delicate areas of concern; the CSR program appears to lack sensitivity to the overall impact of the corporation.

Lockheed Martin ethics officers respond to this concern by pointing out that it is not possible for every set of corporate activities to come under the auspices of the ethics office. Furthermore, they say, the corporation has to trust that the existing ethics program will encourage employees to apply company principles to all aspects of their work, including the impact on local communities. At some point, an ethics program should empower people to do their best, not simply police them.

Trusting people to do their best, however, makes the most sense when the issues are simple, and where a single individual has enough information and capacity to make the best possible decision. The relationship between one of Lockheed Martin's businesses and its surrounding community, however, is a complex and dynamic network of exchanges, likely to involve hundreds of people in different capacities. Each individual may undertake his or her part with the utmost care and conscientiousness, but the sum total of their actions may still do harm in unintended and unforeseeable ways—unforeseeable, that is, if there is no framework in place to encourage a collective understanding and analysis of the ethical dimensions of the corporation's relationship with the community.

For Lockheed Martin, the segregation of the ethics program from larger questions of policy and mission is especially sensitive, given the nature of the corporation's business. After all, Lockheed Martin makes money by designing, manufacturing, and servicing machines that destroy property and human life. Indeed, these machines have been put to extensive use in the past decade, as the high-tech American military of the late twentieth and early twenty-first centuries has been deployed in the Middle East and around the world. Making money on fighter planes, missiles, and spy equipment puts the company squarely up against the American tradition of discomfort with the ethics of war profits. Lockheed Martin's ethics program is entirely silent on the moral dimensions of its core business. As long as it refuses to engage its constituencies about this crucial issue in an honest and sophisticated manner, Lockheed Martin will remain the subject of suspicion and hostility among a broad cross section of the American public.

As in the past, the debate over the ethics of weapons manufacturing is cast today in the starkest terms. Critics of weapons manufacturers portray the industry as corrupt, self-interested, and heartless; the "merchants of death" theory is still alive and well, all the more invigorated by the size of the corporations and the size of the weapons that they make today. On the other hand, supporters of the defense industry tend to insinuate that raising questions about the morality of the business is subversive and un-American.

Deliberately outrageous in its presentation for the "prosecution," but typical in its content, is Michael's Moore's treatment of Lockheed Martin in his 2003 film *Bowling for Columbine*. The documentary explores the landscape of American violence, drawing provocative but casual connections between the attitudes of gun lovers, the actions of the American military, and the motivations of manufacturers of weapons. Lockheed Martin is one of Moore's favorite targets, since it happens that the corporation is one of the principal employers in Littleton, Colorado, the site of the deadly shootings at Columbine High School. For Moore, the presence of the defense industry giant is no coincidence. He films trucks laden with long-range missiles rolling through the streets of Littleton in the middle of the night, and he challenges a nervous Lockheed Martin public relations representative at the factory about how he feels about making weapons of mass destruction. No wonder, Moore suggests, that our children feel they have license to pick up guns and unload on their classmates, when they live in a community where destruction by the ton is the principal source of employment and pride. Throughout the whole film, Moore keeps returning to Lockheed Martin as a convenient symbol and target. In another sequence, he blames the corporation's participation in the welfare-to-work field for a tragic incident where a six-year-old boy is shot while playing with an unattended handgun; the boy was left alone, Moore suggests, because the Lockheed Martin program forced his mother into an unnaturally long commute. The picture is clear. In Moore's diatribe, Lockheed Martin is a soulless corporate giant, cynically peddling violence on a global scale, and directly contributing to a culture of wanton killing within the United States.

Lockheed Martin has an equally one-dimensional perspective on the ethical dimensions of its core activities: We are in the freedom business. From the corporation's point of view, its products deter violence, rather than instigate it. Moreover, the defense industry simply serves the needs and demands of a democratically elected federal government. When I tell Brian Sears that some people I know consider ethics in the weapons business to be something of an oxymoron, he bristles. He reminds me that Lockheed Martin is part of the defense industry, with an emphasis on *defense*. "It is not unethical for a country to defend itself," he says, jolted a bit from his usual laid-back manner. "The opposite is closer to the case. It is unethical for a country *not* to defend itself. If someone is breaking into your house, would it be ethical to shoot him? I can say this for sure: If someone were breaking into my house and I had a gun (which I don't, by the way), I would have no qualms about shooting that person. Not to defend my family would be irresponsible, immoral, and indefensible."

Sears is proud, he goes on, of Lockheed Martin's contributions to the country, and he is realistic about their impact. "I know that our products have been used in battle. I know that our products kill people. Hopefully, it's the bad guys who are being killed. I simply don't view our products as immoral. Even though our products kill people, it's killing people in the service of protecting ourselves." Sears understands that the corporation has and will continue to have its critics. "We're never going to be warm, fuzzy friends with Greenpeace or any other group that's for peace at all costs. The Sisters of St. Francis are never going to love us. They'll buy their 100 shares of stock and show up at our shareholders' meeting and say their thing. And that's fine. The peace activists will never like what we do. We understand their position. We just don't agree with it."

There is something profoundly unsatisfying about this debate, or rather, about this lack of a debate. Moore makes an unambiguous (and sometimes sophomoric) case that the weapons business is inherently corrupt, that the industry has a stake in the demand for killing machines that makes manufacturers morally responsible for the deaths those machines cause. His is the modern variant of the "merchants of death" position that gripped the nation in the 1930s. Sears and Lockheed Martin, for their part, make a case for the inherent righteousness of the defense industry's cause, for weapons systems as an indispensable tool of liberty. Both parties seem to insist that there is no possible discussion, no avenue for conversation between the corporation and its critics on this crucial issue.

But what, after all, is an ethics program *for,* if it is going to put aside altogether the questions at the very heart of the organization? Without judging the merits of the case, it seems unarguable that there are profound ethical questions about the nature of the weapons business that deserve sustained attention. What responsibilities do weapons makers have for how their products are used? To whom should those products be sold, and under what circumstances? Do weapons manufacturers directly or indirectly contribute to causes of warfare by generating the need and demand for their products? What is the collateral impact on the larger culture of investing so heavily in massive military systems?

From Lockheed Martin's point of view, there are two principal reasons—one stated, one unstated—why questions like these are off the table. The stated reason is that, after all, Lockheed Martin's ultimate responsibility as a defense contractor is to serve the interests of the U.S. government. "At Lockheed Martin, we never forget who we're working for," is one of the corporation's most oft-cited mottoes. The ethical considerations, in other words, belong to the client, not to the manufacturer. As long as the corporation follows the law scrupulously and observes fair business practices in selling to the American military, it is fulfilling its ethical obligations both to the letter and in spirit. Questions about how and whether the weapons are used, who has access to which systems, the prosecution of warfare, collateral damage to civilian populations—these are considerations for the military and civilian leadership of the nation, not for the private sector. Of course, Lockheed Martin has both a legal and ethical obligation to be extremely careful when selling its products to customers *other* than the U.S. government—but those situations most definitely *are* treated extensively in the corporation's ethics program, in units regarding the protection of proprietary and classified information, rules for dealing with foreign governments, and related issues. When it comes to selling to the U.S. military, however, the corporation's only real ethical obligation is to provide the best and most reliable products.

The unstated reason is that no organization wants to take the risk of opening up sensitive questions about its fundamental reason for being. Lockheed Martin has been in the weapons business for a very long time, and it has developed a tradition and culture built around excelling in that field. It is perfectly fine for critics from outside to voice their concerns, but no corporation has an obligation to examine itself into extinction.

There are merits to both of these reasons for silence on the ethics of weapons making. It is quite true that moral considerations about the use of force lie in the domain of military, more than corporate, ethics. Furthermore, it is difficult for any high-powered organization to do its work with the speed and vigor necessary to pursue excellence if its members are wondering too much about whether what they are doing is, in the end, "right." Indeed, to the contrary, Lockheed very much depends on the moral certainty of patriotism as one important incentive for employees to work their hardest and their best to meet crucial deadlines. Philosophical musings might very well undermine the zeal that enables this corporation to do its best work.

Yet silence on this core issue threatens the integrity and the credibility of the entire ethics program. Whoever buys its products, Lockheed Martin helps to make some of the deadliest man-made objects on the face of the earth. To claim that this fact has no ethical implications for the manufacturer is, on the face of it, absurd. Loss of civilian life and other forms of "collateral damage"; the dangers to humankind posed by the manufacture of nuclear missiles; the social costs of an enormous defense budget—while many people and organizations may share responsibility for these issues, it is difficult to argue that the corporation that makes the products bears no ethical responsibility for their consequences. This does not mean that the company should abandon its core mission, but it does mean that it is difficult to take seriously the depth of its commitment to ethics if this issue cannot even be discussed.

Passing the ethical issues along to the government is an evasion of responsibility, especially in an interconnected world in which the relationship between the corporation and the government is much more than provider and client. If individual employees tried to avoid hard questions about their own ethical dilemmas by sloughing them off on the actions of supervisors or coworkers or the demands of the customer, they would run afoul of company values. If honesty and integrity and respect are going to mean something at the individual level, they must mean something at the institutional level as well.

Blind allegiance to the corporation's largest customer, by the way, may ultimately lead to its own problems. The corruption scandals of the 1980s were not the result of a handful of renegade employees, but of a system of glad-handing and favoritism involving both the government and the private sector. Misdeeds were implicitly justified by the patriotic imperative to build up the country's defenses in order to win the Cold War. Compliance with the letter and spirit of the laws and regulations of the United States is certainly important. But companies like Lockheed Martin would also do well to maintain a watchful eye on the ethical dimensions of the very laws, regulations, and procedures of the government itself. The U.S. government has uncovered many scandals, but it has spawned them as well. A defense contractor has a better chance of protecting itself if it keeps core questions open, rather than closing them off.

The controversy over Halliburton's role in the Iraq War and its aftermath in 2003 and 2004 illustrates this problem vividly. The defense services company won a series of large contracts from the U.S. government related to the rebuilding of Iraq, but found itself the target of scathing public criticism on two fronts. First, Vice-President Dick Cheney had served for several years as Halliburton's CEO, leading to widespread speculation that Halliburton had directly or indirectly traded on Cheney's influence to win the contracts. Second, in an echo of the "warhogs" debates of the twentieth century, Halliburton was accused of making excessive profits on some of its services, essentially taking advantage of a wartime climate to obtain unfair advantage. Halliburton is a signatory of the Defense Industry Initiative, and the corporation has all the key elements of an ethics and business conduct program. But if anything, the existence of these programs simply made Halliburton a more inviting target for public criticism, because it made the appearance of the gap between principles and actions seem all the greater.[9]

One way that a defense contractor might narrow the gap between principles and action is through public discussion of the moral and ethical dimensions of specific choices in defense policy and weapons systems. This, after all, is the way that other industries have begun to weave ethics into policy, without undermining their core mission. The automobile industry does not grind to a halt because of ethical concerns over 55,000 deaths a year in the United States. Car manufacturers have, however, made safety concerns a part of their public discourse—partly under pressure from the government, partly for marketing reasons, and partly out of a growing internal sense of responsibility. The defense industry can likewise participate in public discussions about its own strategic decisions as well as decisions of the federal government, without damaging the case for its own existence.

In an industry where competition and collaboration with other corporations is a way of life, dealing with the ethical macro-issues might best be handled collectively. The Defense Industry Initiative (DII) was a groundbreaking idea in 1986, when a group of fierce competitors came together to address collectively the series of business practice scandals that had beset their industry. Over the past two decades, the DII has served as the nation's most creative industry consortium, nurturing a spirit of commitment to excellence in ethics programs and to full-fledged values efforts. The DII is strong enough to take on more than just administrative ethics. Together, the major corporations in the defense industry could take a lead in embracing and confronting the full range of ethics questions that face their industry, in partnership with the federal government itself. What kinds of weapons does the United States need? What are the moral and ethical implications of manufacturing, or of *not* manufacturing, certain weapons systems? Can certain manufacturing capabilities be put to nonmilitary use? Together with its competitors, who are its partners in the DII, Lockheed Martin could help transform the nature of public debate over the defense industry. Indeed, it could help create a reasoned debate, in place of the strident polemics that characterize the discourse today.

In summary, there are at least four directions that Lockheed Martin could pursue in integrating ethics in its fullest sense into the enterprise:

1. A more formal role for senior ethics officers in strategic and policy decisions would be an important first step. Informal consultation is no substitute for "a seat at the table."

2. The corporation could build a bridge between its ethics programs and its efforts in the area of corporate social responsibility. That framework of that bridge need not be burdensome. There is no reason for ethics programs to become ethics empires. But the clear line at Lockheed Martin between ethics and social responsibility suggests a habit of segregation that threatens to undermine the ultimate effectiveness of both endeavors. The divorce between "ethics" and "corporate social responsibility" may make sense in terms of the bureaucracy, but it makes no sense at all in terms of a strand of public thinking that sees business ethics in terms of a corporation's role amid its neighbors.

3. Lockheed Martin can make the ethical dimension of discussion of specific business decisions part of its public discourse. Such openness would go a long way toward combating public cynicism and hostility toward the defense industry, which has heightened in the wake of accusations regarding business practices during the Iraq War.

4. The corporation can take a leadership role in urging the DII to expand on its outstanding role in business practice, and to take on the thornier issues of the ethical dimensions of the defense industry as a whole. This kind of leadership would ultimately pay off in better decision making for the nation, which would in turn pay dividends in more credibility and more dependable business relationships in the industry itself.

Raising questions about the corporation's core business need not undermine the entire program. After all, people who adopt Michael Moore's perspective simply will not work at Lockheed Martin. But having the confidence to face these questions directly, allowing for a flexible give and take, and developing a more nuanced vocabulary for discussing the corporation's core business would strengthen every part of the ethics enterprise. By raising and tackling the largest questions honestly, the company would send a signal that it expects similar depth and courage in facing the full range of ethics issues that each of its employees confronts. Lockheed Martin is not about to abandon the weapons industry, nor would consideration of the ethical complexities of that industry lead it to do so. But it would be a stronger, more vibrant, more credible corporate citizen if it had the courage to search for a more supple approach to discussing both the opportunities and the perils of its mission.[10]

Lockheed Martin offers a case study in American virtue. By the standards of its industry, its ethics organization is doing an exemplary job. It has produced a sturdy and innovative program that introduces important concepts to the whole organization, reinforces a consistent message, and generates a concerted effort to strengthen fidelity to appropriate standards of business conduct. Yet for all its successes, two nagging questions remain. First, has the corporation fully addressed the root causes of potential ethics issues? And second, do the corporation's programs measure and address the corporation's full impact on the wider world?

The Lockheed Martin ethics program echoes one of the oldest American stories: the tale of one so confident and secure about his competence and righteousness that he makes himself vulnerable to the dangers that lurk in the world, and the evil that lies within himself. Americans like to think of themselves as upright, but they are often loathe to look at the larger picture of their circumstances: the gross inequalities that persist despite the rhetoric of equality; instances of greed masked in complicated financial reports; violence done in the name of keeping the peace. Americans live in a society that has become expert at presenting a moral face, while defining morality so narrowly that they are constantly letting themselves off the hook when it comes to the larger issues of justice and fairness. Lockheed Martin's program exemplifies this spirit: Its dedicated ethics officers pursue their work with innovation and diligence, but no one is asking or permitting them to take on the larger picture. It is threatening to do so, but it is equally dangerous to ignore the big questions, which have a way of creating disruptions at unexpected moments.

This tension has long-standing roots in American history and culture. One particularly dramatic rendition of that tale, although it is nearly 150 years old, vividly illustrates how fine the line is between triumph and catastrophe.

In his 1856 novella *Benito Cereno*, Herman Melville tells the story of Amasa Delano, captain of an American trading ship, who comes across a mysterious, half-wrecked Spanish vessel, the *San Dominick*, floating off the coast of South America. Delano and his crew board the ship, where they find its captain, Don Benito Cereno, in a puzzling state of apathy. Don Benito tells the Americans a long and complicated story of storms, disease, and death en route from Africa, where they picked up a cargo of Black slaves. Delano looks around the ship and is disgusted by what he sees: a slovenly, decaying vessel where the Spanish sailors mope around indifferently, and where the Blacks, equally sullen, appear slow to obey the commands of the crew. Delano is particularly affronted by the liberties taken by a slave named Babo, Don Benito's personal attendant, who strikes the American captain as lurking on the brink of insubordination. The American captain can draw only one conclusion from what he sees aboard the *San Dominick:* The tribulations of the voyage have somehow dimmed the minds and capacities of Don Benito and his men.

At a crucial moment, however, Delano's perceptions are turned upside down, as the Blacks aboard the ship cast off their chains, take up arms, and attack the American boarding party. The instant reveals that the situation aboard the Spanish ship has been an elaborate sham: The

Blacks, not the Spanish, have all along been in charge, led by that very Babo who appeared to wait so obsequiously upon Don Benito. Weeks earlier, the slaves had successfully risen against the crew, killing most, and demanding that they be taken back to Africa. Delano and his men manage to strike back, bring the ship under control, and restore order and the proper authority, but the American captain remains puzzled by how the situation aboard the slaver could have gone so awry.

The point is that Delano could not imagine an alternative reality outside of his rigid moral framework. He had a clear-cut view of social structure and authority: On board a ship, a captain is in charge, and everyone is subject to his orders. Members of the crew carry out their assigned tasks, and if one gets out of line, he is punished accordingly. People generally act for the best, as long as their instructions are clearly and fairly delivered. Arriving aboard the Spanish ship, Amasa Delano placed his faith in human nature, in the radiant power of his ship and his country, and in his own intuition. Presented with a set of mysterious circumstances—ominous drumming, slinking shadows, and odd behaviors—he can interpret them only in terms of his existing worldview: He sees weakness in the Spaniards, rather than strength in the Blacks. His blindness to the reality of his circumstances, to a system of power and motivation outside the boundaries of the world as he knows it, nearly costs him his ship and his life. He simply cannot envisage a situation where the Blacks are in charge.

Even after this disillusioning experience, Delano remains upbeat, trying to talk a depressed Don Benito Cereno back to cheerfulness. Delano *has* drawn a lesson from this experience: Evil can lurk beneath the surface of appearances. Those who appeared to be docile slaves turned out, in the end, to be murderous savages. The American captain will be more careful in the future, perhaps. His fundamental outlook, however, remains intact.

The reader realizes, however, with Benito Cereno, that Captain Delano has completely missed the point of his own experience. Delano believes that evil lay in the murderous nature of the Africans. We recognize, however, that Delano is blind to the real evil: the legal trafficking in human lives that is fundamental to the social and economic life of his country. The slaves may have been murderous indeed, but we cannot judge their violence outside of the context of the violence that has been done to them. Delano never sees this. He cannot penetrate beneath the surface of events because he lacks the capacity and the will to question the moral framework in which he operates. He is a thoroughly decent, upstanding, good-hearted citizen and soldier whose ethical system operates within strict and impermeable boundaries. His inability to stretch those boundaries nearly cost him his life, but he seems doomed to repeat the experience in other circumstances, because he has failed to absorb the lesson of the *San Dominick.*

Delano's mind set is the habit of American virtue: We trust in our own fundamental decency. We consider moral questions in a tightly controlled sphere. And we assume that evil is an aberration, something outside ourselves, something to be fought and challenged and conquered when at last it rears its head. Ethics focuses on individual behavior within our sphere, rather than addressing challenging questions about the nature of the social or organizational enterprise itself.

This mindset is not limited to corporate America. It also characterizes our political life, at both ends of the ideological spectrum. We tend to construct moral systems that appear wholly consistent from within, but are impervious to the perspective of the wider world. Sometimes this can take the form of a U.S. crusade to bring liberty and enlightenment to distant parts of the world, with little respect for indigenous viewpoints about how best to construct a fair and just society. Sometimes this can take the form of a crusade to purge American life of bigotry, its partisans unable to see the consequences of their own forms of intolerance. A values-based corporation, a democratic world, a tolerant nation—it is easy to be swept up in the nobility of the ideals, and to evade the less pleasant task of searching self-examination.

Much can be accomplished this way. Melville suggests that Delano's ship was a model of efficiency and decorum, expertly managed within its domain. So, too, Lockheed Martin's ethics program is in many ways a splendid model. The corporation has been a leader in bringing a formal consideration of ethics issues into the very center of its enterprise. Not only is Lockheed Martin a better organization for those efforts; through cooperative arrangements, its programs have had a salutary effect on others both inside and outside of the defense industry.

The sheer earnestness of Lockheed Martin's ethics program is remarkable. The men and women like Dave Sanders and Brian Sears and

Wendy Donaldson who make up the company's ethics team have produced a program with a clear sense of mission, and have imbued the company with a remarkable esprit de corps. Their ethics program is neatly packaged and scrupulously documented, with "contacts" counted by the thousand. In the decade since the mega-merger created Lockheed Martin, the company has managed to escape sensational scandal. Its ethics program has been hailed for its innovations and its scope. Its efforts in this area have been copied by its competitors, and the corporation has been hailed (and rewarded) by its largest customer, the U.S. government, for its improvements in this area. By this yardstick, Lockheed Martin's programs have been a terrific success.

But there is also something chilling about the tidiness of the corporation's ethics package. The game boxes are clever and attractive; the cases to discuss are thoughtful and well-balanced. The flowcharts that illustrate the investigations process are clear and unambiguous. The survey data are splendidly thorough and quantified. All this tidiness, however, seems out of step with the business of human malfeasance, in all its messiness and complexity. By its very nature, ethics resists completion and closure. Rules and codes and cases tend to reduce ethics to a checklist, rather than to a process of self-examination that explores gray areas and intractable dilemmas. To their credit, Brian Sears and others at Lockheed Martin have recognized this, and have tried to incorporate complexity into their program through emphasizing multiple "perspectives" on problems. The corporate culture of problem solving, however, is irresistible. It is hard to resist the conclusion that, in the end, Lockheed Martin's executives are most comfortable with a kind of ethics engineering, flawless in design, but not necessarily so perfect in the unpredictable circumstances of real-world conditions.

Lockheed Martin has created the tidiness of its ethics program by building it inside a sturdy compartment and then carefully making sure that the package remains intact. This is a careful strategy, aiming to build morale within the Lockheed Martin community, and to build confidence about the ethics program among those who work for the U.S. government and in the larger arena of public opinion. This strategy does not diminish the program's successes within that compartment. But it does mean that the program will inevitably meet at best only a portion of public expectations, because not everyone accepts the notion that ethics should be so strictly contained. If business ethics means the full measure of the impact that a corporation has on its world, then compartmentalizing an ethics program will always be unsatisfactory. A narrowly defined ethics program may thwart hackers, cheaters, and thieves, but it is poorly positioned to consider and prevent the greatest harms that a powerful organization can inflict on its communities, and on the world.

With all that Lockheed Martin's ethics program has accomplished in the last fifteen years, it may seem unfair to chide the corporation about what lies outside the "box": attention to the specific challenges faced by senior management; the ethics of collective decision making; the interface between ethics and social responsibility; and the ethics of the core enterprise itself. But the challenge lies precisely in the corporation's success. What it has accomplished inside the box is so substantial that it has the effect of strengthening the box itself. What is inside gets more treatment, more attention, more clever additions like online "infomercials" and film festivals. The matters beyond the box become more distant, major questions that are someone else's problem.

Corporations in the United States have changed the face of the world through innovations in engineering, marketing, and business practice. Can they bring this same spirit to embracing a fuller conception of an "organizational culture" built on ethics? This is the next test of American power.

Notes

Introduction: In the Shadow of the Skunk Works (pages 1-17)

1. At the request of Lockheed Martin, the names of corporation employees, other than those who work at corporate headquarters, the winners of the Ethics Film Festival, and the winners of the Lockheed Martin Chairman's Award (see chapter 3), have been changed to pseudonyms.

2. The Sarbanes–Oxley Act of 2002, P.L. 107–204.

3. The guidelines and explanatory materials can be found on the web site of the United States Sentencing Commission: www.ussc.gov.

4. Recent titles include: Mimi Swartz with Sherron Watkins, *Power Failure: The Inside Story of the Collapse of Enron* (New York: Doubleday, 2003); Barbara Ley Toffler with Jennifer Reingold, *Final Accounting: Ambition, Greed and the Fall of Arthur Andersen* (New York: Broadway Books, 2003); Frank Partnoy, *Infectious Greed: How Deceit and Risk Corrupted the Financial Markets* (New York: Times Books, 2003); Robert Bryce, *Pipe Dreams: Greed, Ego and the Death of Enron* (New York: Public Affairs, 2002).

5. Dawn-Marie Driscoll and W. Michael Hoffman, *Ethics Matters: How to Implement Values-Driven Management* (Waltham, Mass.: Center for Business Ethics, 2000).

6. Lynn Sharp Paine, *Value Shift* (New York: McGraw-Hill, 2003).

7. Mike W. Martin, *Meaningful Work: Rethinking Professional Ethics* (New York: Oxford University Press, 2000).

8. Howard Gardner, Mihaly Csikszentmihalyi, and William Damon, *Good Work: When Excellence and Ethics Meet* (New York: Basic Books, 2001).

Chapter One: Titans and Warhogs (pages 18-48)

1. Lockheed Martin, *Setting the Standard: Code of Ethics and Business Conduct* (March 2003), 1.

2. Bernard Bailyn, "The Apologia of Robert Keayne," *The William and Mary Quarterly* 7, no. 4 (October 1950), 568–587.

3. See Jesper Rosenmeier, "John Cotton on Usury," *William and Mary Quarterly,* 47, no. 4 (October 1990), 548–565.

4. Peter Baida, *Poor Richard's Legacy: American Business Values from Benjamin Franklin to Donald Trump* (New York: William Morrow, 1990), 69.

5. Baida, *Poor Richard's Legacy,* 126.

6. Theodore Dreiser, *The Titan* (New York: John Lane and Sons, 1914), 251–255.

7. "Note Left Juror 'Very, Very Scared'" *New York Daily News,* 8 April, 2004, 19.

8. Saul Engelbourg, *Power and Morality: American Business Ethics, 1840–1914* (Westport, Conn.: Greenwood Press, 1980), 15–16.

9. Engelbourg, *Power and Morality,* 27.

10. Edgar L. Heermance, *The Ethics of Business: A Study of Current Standards* (New York: Harper & Brothers, 1926), 50.

11. See Morton Keller, *The Life Insurance Enterprise, 1885–1910: A Study in the Limits of Corporate Power* (Cambridge, Mass.: Harvard University Press, 1963), 245–264.

12. W. Wallace Kirkpatrick, "The Adequacy of Internal Corporate Controls," in Arthur S. Miller, ed., *The Ethics of Business Enterprise* (Philadelphia: American Academy of Political and Social Science, 1962), 77–80.

13. Heermance, *The Ethics of Business,* 163–172.

14. Harold C. Livesay, *Andrew Carnegie and the Rise of Big Business* (Boston: Little, Brown, 1975).

15. Thomas Dublin, *Women at Work: The Transformation of Work and Community in Lowell, Massachusetts, 1826–1860* (New York: Columbia University Press, 1979).

16. Irving Bernstein, *The Lean Years* (Boston: Houghton Mifflin, 1960), chapter 3.

17. Stephen Meyer III, *The Five Dollar Day: Labor Management and Social Control in the Ford Motor Company, 1908–1921* (Albany: State University of New York Press, 1981), 73–74.

18. Meyer, *The Five Dollar Day,* 127.

19. Meyer, *The Five Dollar Day,* 136–137.

20. Meyer, *The Five Dollar Day,* 123.

21. See David Brody, "The Rise and Decline of Welfare Capitalism," in *Workers in Industrial America: Essays on the Twentieth Century Struggle* (New York: Oxford University Press, 1980), 48–81, and Stuart D. Brandes, *American Welfare Capitalism, 1880–1940* (Chicago: University of Chicago Press, 1976).

22. Sanford M. Jacoby, *Modern Manors: Welfare Capitalism since the New Deal* (Princeton, N.J.: Princeton University Press, 1997).

23. Howard R. Bowen, *Social Responsibilities of the Businessman* (New York: Harper & Brothers, 1953), 52–53.

24. Bowen, *Social Responsibilities of the Businessman,* 68.

25. Bowen, *Social Responsibilities of the Businessman,* 76, 117.

26. Roland Marchand, *Creating the Corporate Soul: The Rise of Public Relations and Corporate Imagery in American Big Business* (Berkeley: University of California Press, 1998), 64–67 and passim.

27. Stuart D. Brandes, *Warhogs: A History of War Profits in America* (Lexington: University Press of Kentucky, 1997), 38.

28. Brandes, *Warhogs,* 102.

29. Brandes, *Warhogs,* 224.

Chapter Two: Success and Scandal (pages 49–75)

1. This account relies on the most comprehensive one-volume history of the Lockheed Corporation, covering the period before the merger with Martin Marietta, which is Walter J. Boyne, *Beyond the Horizons: The Lockheed Story* (New York: St. Martin's Press, 1998). A timeline of Lockheed Martin history can also be found on the corporation's web site at www.lockheedmartin.com.

2. The most complete source on the Lockheed scandals of the 1950s, 1960s, and 1970s is David Boulton, *The Lockheed Papers* (London: Jonathan Cape, 1978).

3. "Lockheed Ex-official Says that Initiative in Bribe Cases Came from Japanese," *New York Times,* 20 December 1976, 8; "Kotchian Calls Himself Scapegoat," *New York Times,* 3 July 1997, 73.

4. "Congress to Investigate Increase in Cost of C-5A Plane," *New York Times,* 1 December 1968, S15; "A New Attack on Waste in Defense Spending," *New York Times,* 22 June, 1969, E4.

5. John Kenneth Galbraith, "The Big Defense Firms Are Really Public Firms and Should Be Nationalized," *New York Times Sunday Magazine,* 16 November 1969, 50.

6. Andy Pasztor, *When the Pentagon Was for Sale: Inside America's Biggest Defense Scandal* (New York: Scribner, 1995), 29–31.

7. Quoted in Pasztor, *When the Pentagon Was for Sale,* 92.

8. President's Blue Ribbon Commission on Defense Spending, *A Quest for Excellence* (June 1986). Available at www.ndu.edu/library/pbrc/pbrc.html.

9. See the web site of the Defense Industry Initiative at www.dii.org.

10. "Lockheed Pleads Guilty to Bribery Conspiracy; Firm Agrees to Pay $24.8 Million in Fines," *Washington Post,* 28 January 1995, C1.

11. Norman R. Augustine, *Augustine's Travels* (New York: American Management Association, 1998), 17–37.

12. Norman Augustine, *Augustine's Laws*, (Reston, Va.: American Institute of Aeronautics and Astronautics, 1997), 23.

13. Augustine, *Augustine's Laws*, 36–37.

14. This case appears in the 1998 "Ethics Challenge," which followed a format nearly identical to the 1997 version.

Chapter Three: Peeling Back the Onion *(pages 76-116)*

1. An overview of the structure and organization of the ethics and business conduct program is available at www.lockheedmartin.com.

2. Warren Rudman et al., "A Report to the Chairman and Board of Directors of The Boeing Company concerning the company's ethics program and its rules and procedures for the treatment of competitors' proprietary information" (November 3, 2003), 59. Available at www.boeing.com.

3. Lockheed Martin Corporation, *Setting The Standard: Code of Ethics and Business Conduct* (March 2003). Capitalization is in the original.

4. Corporations have taken a variety of approaches to ethics training programs in recent years. Most of the major defense contractors now also have at least the hour per year training that Lockheed Martin offers. But some companies have developed more intensive formats. Sun Microsystems, for example, now regularly puts its managers through an intensive two-day ethics "boot camp." See "Boot Camps on Ethics Ask the 'What Ifs?'" *New York Times*, 5 January 2003, 18.

5. These figures track the most extensive national survey of workers very closely. See *National Business Ethics Survey 2003* (Washington, D.C.: Ethics Resource Center, 2003), chapters 4 and 6.

6. The results of the corporation's 2003 survey were, by and large, consistent with the 2001 results. New questions about the responsiveness of supervisors to reports of misconduct were included; these showed that approximately 30 percent of those who reported misconduct to their supervisors were less than fully satisfied with the response. No doubt the corporation will be tracking those numbers in future surveys, to measure the success of "Ethical Tools for Leaders." *Lockheed Martin Today* (March 2004), 5–8.

7. The web site of the Ethics Officers Association is www.eoa.org.

8. Both reports, "A Report to the Chairman and Board of Directors of The Boeing Company Concerning the Company's Ethics Program and Its Rules and Procedures for the Treatment of Competitors' Proprietary Information" (3 November 2003) and "A Report to the Chairman and Board of Directors of The Boeing Company Concerning the Company's Policies and Practices for the Hiring of Government and Former Government Employees" (26 February 2004),

are available at www.boeing.com. Also at the Boeing web site is the executive summary of a report by the Ethical Leadership Group titled "The Boeing Company: An Assessment of the Ethics Program."

9. Andy Meisler, "Lockheed Is Doing Right and Doing Well," *Workforce Management On-Line,* March 2004. Available at www.workforce.com/section/09/feature/23/65/12/index_printer.html.

Chapter Four: Vulnerabilities (pages 117-154)

1. "Pentagon Brass and Military Contractors' Gold," *New York Times,* 29 June, 2004, C1.

2. W. Michael Hoffman and Dawn-Marie Driscoll, "Business Ethics in the New Millennium: Will the Patient Survive?" *Business Ethics Quarterly* 10, no. 1 (2000), 221–231.

3. The full Federal Contractor Misconduct Database can be found at the website for Project on Governmental Oversight (www.pogo.org).

4. "United States Announces Settlement of Lockheed Martin Case, Alleging Mischarging on Government Contracts," press release, 27 August, 2003 (www.usdoj.gov).

5. "Wages of Sin: Why Lawbreakers still win government contracts," *U.S. News and World Report,* 13 May 2002, 28; "Are Corporations Too Big to Debar?" *Wall Street Journal,* 10 June 2003, 6.

6. As of fall 2004, Lockheed Martin officials say that they have developed an ethical maturity assessment tool that addresses this suggestion.

7. In 2004, the Equal Employment Opportunity Commission (EEOC) found that officials at the Meridien facility had responded inadequately to a pattern of racist threats by Doug Williams over a period of eighteen months before the shootings, and that African American employees continued to face a hostile working environment in its aftermath. "Company Cited in Worker Killings," *New York Times,* 13 July 2004, A14.

8. When presented with my concerns about the relationship of diversity and ethics, Lockheed Martin officials responded in writing as follows:

Diversity at Lockheed Martin is about a great deal more than just our product line, our heritage, or the acceptance of just a "long-haired engineer"; however, that is part of it. We believe diversity includes everyone and we are committed to being supportive and inclusive to our employees as a must in achieving mission success. Diversity is a business imperative, as minority populations within the U.S. continue to grow, amd college-educated graduates with technical degrees continue on the decline, we must be attractive to a broad array of qualified, diverse job candidates. We are aware of the challenges in encouraging students to pursue technical fields, so we are taking action (these are just two examples of a multitude of endowment, outreach and mentorship programs we have throughout the corporation):

- We support 36 community-based organizations designed to enhance career opportunities in engineering, science, and math-based disciplines for women and people of color.
- Lockheed Martin supports and participates in 22 minority educational programs.

9. Dan Baum, "Nation Builders for Hire," *New York Times Magazine,* 22 June 2003, 32.

10. When presented with my concerns about the ethics of the corporation's core business, Lockheed Martin officials responded in writing as follows:

The author suggests that we could do more with our current ethics program to reach beyond our company walls, to address the implications of the products and services that we deliver to our government customers. In sum, one can argue that we develop weapons that promote warfare, while we would argue, like our government customers, that a strong military, outfitted with the some of the most technologically advanced equipment in the world—is the best way to avoid ever having to go to war in the first place. Also, you fail to point out that Lockheed Martin is not just about weapons; in fact, we are the number one supplier of information technology to the federal government. Our technology helps to ensure the delivery of vital government services that all U.S. citizens rely upon, such as the timely arrival of monthly Social Security checks. Your suggestion for us to be in the forefront on the global impact of our business is akin to asking mankind why he has waged war for thousands of years. It is an issue separate from any entity, let alone company. It is an issue shared by all of mankind.